The Disciplines

Tom Graves
Liz Poraj-Wilczynska

Published by
Tetradian Books
Unit 215, 9 St Johns Street,
Colchester, Essex CO2 7NN, England

http://www.tetradianbooks.com

First published: September 2008
ISBN 978-1-906681-08-1 (paperback)
ISBN 978-1-906681-09-8 (e-book)

Contents

Introduction 1

   A bit of background... 1

   An emphasis on quality 2

   Dowsing and beyond 3

   A question of discipline 5

   Killing quality 6

Dowsing in ten minutes 7

   What is dowsing?.. 7

   Know your instrument.. 8

   It's all coincidence.. 13

   What's the need?... 15

   Round the bend... 17

A question of quality 20

   Objective quality 20

   Subjective quality... 21

   Quality in practice 22

The disciplined dowser 25

The dowser as artist..29

   Principles… 29

   …and practice 30

The dowser as mystic 37

   Principles… 37

   …and practice 39

The dowser as scientist 45

   Principles… 45

   …and practice 46

The dowser as magician 53

   Principles… 53

   …and practice 54

The integrated dowser 60

   Principles… 60

   …and practice 61

Seven sins of dubious discipline 65

   The hype hubris 65

   The Golden-Age game 67

   The newage nuisance 69

   The meaning mistake 72

   The possession problem..78

   The reality risk 82

   Lost in the learning labyrinth...87

   Cleansing the sins 89

Practice – enhancing the senses 91

Practice – setup and fieldwork 97

   Preparation 97

   Arriving on site 100

   Fieldwork and records 101

   Closing the session 115

Practice – worked examples 119

   Techniques summary 119

   Belas Knap, Winchcombe, near Cheltenham 120

   Wiggold, near Cirencester 133

Appendix: Resources...139

   Books and text resources 139

   Societies 140

Acknowledgements

Amongst others, the following people kindly provided comments and feedback on the themes and early drafts of this book: Gerry Beskin (London, GB), Colin Clark (Cheltenham, GB), Paul Devereux and Charla Devereux (Cotswolds, GB), Norman Fahy (Castle Rising, GB), Valerie Graves (Colchester, GB), Gordon Ingram (Writtle, GB), Helen Lamb (Malvern, GB), Kevin Masman (Castlemaine, Aus), John Moss (Malvern, GB).

Please note that, to preserve confidentiality, stories and examples have been adapted, combined and in part fictionalised from experiences in a variety of contexts, and (unless otherwise stated) do not and are not intended to represent any specific person or organisation.

INTRODUCTION

A bit of background

A book on dowsing, yes; but why the *disciplines* of dowsing? What's the difference? What's this all about?

Two reasons, really.. The first is that whilst there are plenty of good beginner-level books on dowsing, there are very few that go beyond that beginner stage. And almost all of those are on the general lines of "I did it my way" – which is interesting, of course, but not much help for identifying general principles from which we can improve the quality of dowsing work. This book aims to fill that gap.

In case you don't know dowsing at all, we've included a brief introduction here – see *Dowsing in ten minutes*, on p.7. But after that we'll go straight into principles – the four core disciplines of dowsing, and the bridges between them – and show you how to adapt them in your own working practice.

The second reason for this book is around the need for *quality* in dowsing. Between us we've been involved in various aspects of the field for a fair few decades now: and it's painfully clear that far too much of the dowsing work being done at present – especially in the study of earth-energies and the 'earth-mysteries' field in general – is of dubious quality at best. To be rather less polite about it, much of it is meaningless junk. Kind of pointless, really…

No matter how good the showmanship may be, we cannot escape the fact that quality depends on adherence to some basic rules and guidelines: and if the guidelines are ignored, the results cannot be anything other than rubbish. Which is a problem: a *big* problem. So here we'll not only describe the guidelines – those Four Disciplines of Dowsing, and the links between them – but show you how to verify the quality of your work, and avoid the Seven Sins of Dubious Discipline. It's only then that dowsing becomes *useful*.

In a sense, though, none of this is specific to dowsing. These concerns about principles, adaptation and quality are generic to all skills – especially those with a large subjective component. As one frustrated friend put it the other day, "I've had all these experiences and done all these trainings – shamanic journeys, earth magic, healing groups, meditation, ritual, spirit guides, animal energies, all that stuff – but what do I *do* with it? What's the *use*?" One answer is just to *celebrate* it – enjoy it, accept it for what it is, and leave it at that. In other words, leave it in what we describe later as the modes of 'artist' or 'mystic'. But to *use* it, to *do* something with it, in what we'd call the 'magician' mode, requires a purpose, a direction, a reason – and better quality.

In essence, if we're going to get anywhere useful, we need to get beyond the dilettante 'taster', and *commit* to the skill. As we'll see shortly, we also need to accept that we're going to have to go round the bend a bit in order to go deeper, which in places is not comfortable at all. But that's the only way we're going to lift the quality of the work – and whatever we do, and however we do it, quality really does matter.

An emphasis on quality

Quality sounds *serious*. Don't worry, this isn't that kind of book – it's perfectly okay to have fun and play around! In fact it's not only a good idea, but really important to do so, for a lot of reasons – not least because it's one of the few ways we can get round the fear of failure that would otherwise cripple all of our work. *But* – and it's a big 'but' – what we find there in play is ideas, not facts. We need to *choose* that mode, deliberately, consciously, and *know* that we're in that mode: but *don't* treat the results of that 'play-time' as anything other than the output of the artistic idea-creating space.

There's a place for seriousness, and a place for play. But we need to be *very* clear as to which is which. If not we'll find ourselves on the dreaded New Age 'pub-crawl', full of glamour and grand-iosity, full of excitement and exuberance, but somehow never quite managing to reach a useful outcome – "an empty thunder, signifying nothing".

Where there's reasonable quality, the work has a lot more mean-ing, and it's a lot more fun, too. It's not that hard to create quality, either: much of it comes down to a simple acronym, LEARN – elegant, efficient, appropriate, reliable, integrated. There are some useful tips and tricks, too, that we can draw from the quality-standards used in business: they're from a different context, of course, but as we'll see later, the exact same principles would apply in dowsing and much else besides – and it doesn't take much to adapt them to our purpose here. More on that in the chapter on quality – see *A question of quality*, on p.20.

Dowsing and beyond

So what *is* "our purpose here"? These quality-concerns are not just about dowsing: they apply to any kind of subjective exploration. Yet we'll keep the focus here on dowsing and the 'earth mysteries' field, to give us something specific to work with yet not drown in too many examples or side-excursions. Even if your core interest, though, is in a somewhat different field – healing, perhaps, or the so-called 'psychic' skills – you should still find plenty here that'll be relevant to you, and we'll trust that you'll be able to adapt it to your work as you need.

Let's play with an example here. When we put earth-mysteries studies to practical use, it's called geomancy: feng-shui is perhaps the best-known form of this, though there are many others. It's a broad field, with a very broad scope, but we could summarise how quality impacts on geomancy in generic form as follows:

Quality is a matter of skill. It requires experience – which we don't get just from sitting in an armchair. It requires judgement, aware-ness, dexterity, discernment, even that rarity called 'common sense'. It calls for a good understanding of the mechanics of the problem at hand, the choice of approaches to that problem, and the trade-offs that lead to appropriate methods in any given context. It requires an ability to balance between the content and the context of the problem. And yes, it kind of demands that we go round the bend a bit, in the labyrinthine process of learning each new skill…

Quality is a matter of luck. In feng-shui, for example, they talk about three kinds of luck:

- *heaven-luck* – what happens as a result of our nature, of *who* we are, the milieu in which we live, and so on
- *earth-luck* – what happens because of *where* we are, our surroundings and the like
- *man-luck* – about our choices in finding a balance between heaven-luck and earth-luck, and *how* we use those choices.

So whilst we never have control, we *always* have choice – though there's always a weird twist somewhere in those choices! Murphy's Law is the only real law that there is, but it's so much of a law that it has to apply to itself too – which is where 'man-luck' comes to play. Hence what we might call 'inverse-Murphy': things can go right if we let them – but if we only let them go right in expected ways, we're limiting our chances! Hence too much of geomancy is not only the art of being at the right place at the right time, but *not* being in the wrong place at the wrong time…

Quality is a matter of belief. Let's face it, much of what we do in dowsing, geomancy and the like is pretty crazy, by any ordinary standards. Yet as scientist Stan Gooch put it, there's an important paradox at play here: things not only have to be seen to be believed, but also have to be believed to be seen. In subjective skills, beliefs are *tools*: they play a key role in how well we'll be able to achieve the intended result. But there's a catch, of course. Sometimes things can work – for a while, anyway – because we want them to, or because we've paid the issue some attention: yet if we're not careful about it, when the belief fades, so do the results. And we also need to be *very* careful to learn the boundaries between reality and wishful thinking…

Quality is a matter of context. Rules and guidelines are useful, but *only* useful: we forget that fact at our peril.. Every theory or model expects 'sameness', or at least close similarity; yet every place, everything we deal with, is *itself*, different and distinct. So a key part of geomancy, and the *practice* of dowsing and similar skills, is about knowing to stick to the rule-book, and when to try something else. The rule-books define the likely content; yet in practice it's *context* that determines what will work, and what won't…

Dowsing is a really good test-case for all of this, because there's almost nothing to it other than those subjective skills. (As we'll see in the next chapter, the physical skills we need for dowsing are trivial: you can pick the basics up in a couple of minutes. It's the *rest* of the skill that's not so trivial…) So even if dowsing isn't your usual forte, do have a play with it here: there's much you'll learn that you can apply to *every* skill or discipline.

Which brings us back to this matter of *discipline*: what's all *that* about, you might ask?

A question of discipline

A slight risk of confusion here, perhaps, because we're dealing with two meanings of 'discipline' here – and both of them are valid.

One is the fact of discipline itself, doing things consistently – resolving the mechanics and approaches to that skill, in a manner that's elegant, efficient, appropriate, reliable, integrated. That's the only way we can achieve and maintain quality in our work. More to the point, if we *don't* do that, what we get is rubbish – even if at times we can perhaps try to pretend otherwise… If we want our work to mean something, there's no way to get round this: discipline *matters*.

The catch is that subjective skills such as dowsing depend on a *personal* balance between the mechanics and approaches: there's no predefined "*the* right way to do it" that works for everyone, and certainly no fixed method that covers everything. There are some generic principles that work well – see *A question of quality*, p.20 – but otherwise that's about as close as we get to "*the* method". Beyond that, we need to move up one step to a kind of meta-level, to get to what we might call 'the methods to derive methods'.

This is the other meaning of 'discipline': disciplines – the plural – are what we use to guide the discipline of our work. At the practical level, each kind of work has its own disciplines – the disciplines of water-divining, healing, archaeological survey, earth-energies and so on. What we're interested in here are the disciplines at the next level up, that guide quality and choices within each of the practical disciplines. We could describe the different modes of these 'meta-disciplines' – see *The disciplined dowser*, p.25 – as the Four Disciplines of Dowsing:

- a discipline of *sensing* – see *The dowser as artist*, p.25
- a discipline of *belief* – see *The dowser as mystic*, p.37
- a discipline of *fact* – see *The dowser as scientist*, p.45
- a discipline of *action* – see *The dowser as magician*, p.53

The 'artist' mode is about ideas, experiences, whilst the 'mystic' mode is more about meaning, belonging, deep belief and so on. We also need to link all these different modes together into a unified whole, such that each mode consistently supports the next – see *The integrated dowser*, p.60. We'll show later how all of this comes together, with some detailed worked examples in dowsing and archaeography – see the 'practice' sections, starting at *Practice – enhancing the senses*, p.91.

But if we don't do this in a disciplined way – for example, if we play a random New-Age mix-and-match between the modes – we won't get useful knowledge, we'll get a useless mess. In short, we need to be clear which mode we're in at every moment, and act accordingly – don't mix 'em up!

Killing quality

Mixing the modes is just one of many ways to kill the quality in our work. Some of the (many) others include:

- getting caught up in the hubris and hysteria of *hype*
- losing sense in the quest for some imagined *'Golden Age'*
- indulging in the casual New Age carelessness that we could unkindly call *'newage'*
- making mistakes about the meaning of *meaning*
- trying to cling to certainty and 'truth' by *possession*
- failing to allow for the risks of a *reality* in which 'real' and 'imaginary' can collide in unexpected ways
- skipping over skills-development steps in the labyrinthine process of *learning*

More on all of those later – see *Seven sins of dubious discipline*, p.65. But again, this isn't just about dowsing – it applies in general to anywhere that involves any kind of subjective exploration. For instance, at times we've seen archaeologists come up with some absolute howlers, in terms of ill-thought-through explanations of ancient sites; and most of the attempts by self-styled 'skeptics' to explain dowsing – or, more often, to dismiss it – have been almost text-book examples on how *not* to do science. Discipline matters in *every* discipline.

In our 'practice' sections' starting at *Practice – enhancing the senses*, p.91, we'll cover a broad range of areas, showing how to identify and avoid those mistakes, and maintain discipline whilst moving between the modes. As we'll see, there are a fair few challenges there, and sustaining that discipline does take practice.

But then so does dowsing itself: and in case you're not familiar with that as yet, that's what we need to turn to next.

DOWSING IN TEN MINUTES

Okay, we'll admit it, this might take a bit more than ten minutes – but it'll be quick and easy, anyway.

> And here we'll also put in a shameless plug for some of Tom's other books on dowsing,, such as *The Dowser's Workbook*, *Elements of Pendulum Dowsing* and *The Diviner's Handbook*. The latter has now been in print without a break for more than thirty years, and is still frequently described by others as *the* introduction for beginner-dowsers — try it for yourself, and see!
>
> You'll find publisher-details for these, and for other books we mention, in the 'Resources' appendix on p.139.

What is dowsing?

Dowsing can be found in such a wide variety of forms and with so many different uses – from water-divining to healing, from geomancy to radiesthesia, and a swathe of subtler variants such as 'deviceless dowsing' – that if we look only at the surface appearances it can seem a little difficult to say exactly what it *is*. But if we jump upward a step or two, what they all have in common is this:

- we're *sensing* something (though at the moment don't worry too much about just how or what we're sensing…);
- we have some means to *identify the location* of that sensing (though 'location' can be a pretty broad term here…);
- we have some way – some question in mind – to derive *meaning* from that coincidence ('coincide-ence') of sensing and location;
- the whole point of all this is to put it to some *use*.

Take the example of the stereotype water-diviner – a gnarled old man with a gnarled old stick. The bent twig seems to be part of the process, but its real role is to make it easier both to sense the water below, and to know when he's sensed it. When the rod goes up or down or whatever, that's the right location. X marks the spot. it means there's water there, he says. Which, if you dig down to the right depth, will lead you to water you can use. This isn't a game he's playing: there may well be livelihoods at stake, or lives, even.

And if he's running a full-scale drilling-rig on 'no water, no pay' – as many of the professional water-diviners do – he has another darn good reason to make sure his dowsing is good, too. Quality *matters*.

And let's take another stereotyped example, the distant-healer at her desk, holding a lock of her client's hair in one hand and waggling a pendulum with the other hand over a list of ailments and cures. A twirl of the pendulum one way means 'Yes', she says; the other means 'No'; all the sensing is simplified down to just those two choices. The location here is virtual, or metaphoric: is there a match to *this* place in the body, *this* item on the list? The lock of hair helps her to maintain her focus on *this* specific client – the person to whom this dowsing would be of *use* – which is also, in its way, a kind of location in social space. Put this all together, to derive *meaningful coincidence* – in this case identifying the needs and concerns of the client. Or should be, anyway: the results would be meaningless, even downright dangerous, if the quality of dowsing is poor. Once again, quality *matters*.

Let's jump sideways even further, to an example that at first you might not think of as dowsing: a massage therapist, pressing fingers gently but firmly along the client's arm. The fingers them-selves are the 'dowsing instrument' here, deriving different feel-ings or sensing at specific locations on the arm, or elsewhere in the client's body. What those sensings *mean* to the therapist depends on the conceptual frame in use: it may be physical anatomy, acu-pressure points, auras, whatever – at this metaphoric level they're all much the same. But the aim, the *use* here is to help the client get well, or stay well – there's a practical purpose for all this activity. And the point, once again, is that if the quality isn't there, there's no point in doing the work.

These examples may seem worlds apart, but the underlying prin-ciples are exactly the same: some form of recognisable sensing; an identified location; meaningful coincidence of sensing and location; and a use or purpose for all of this.

See let's look at how all of this works in practice.

Know your instrument

Whenever we go out dowsing on site, there'll always be some spectator who asks "does it *work*, then?" But the question misses the point: *it* doesn't 'work' as such – *you* do. A dowsing instrument – the rod or pendulum or picture-postcard or whatever – can make it easier to see what's going on, but it's not essential: the real instrument is you.

What the visible instruments do is make your own sensing more visible to you. A divining-rod springs up because your hands move slightly. The same with the sideways movements of the angle-rods – as we'll see in a moment. And much the same with the pendulum – the old builders' plumb-bob, or a ring on a string – swinging sideways or in circles because your hand moves slightly fore-and-aft or side to side. So there's nothing special at all: in every case, the instrument moves because your hands move – nothing more than that.

> All right, make that "*almost* every case", because one young woman's version of a pendulum was to get the light-fittings swinging, ten feet above our heads – without touching them. Impressive, if kind of scary...
>
> But that was just one extreme amongst thousands we've known. For the rest of us ordinary mortals, let's stick to Plan A, and keep it simple: the rods move because your hands move!

Let's look at **angle-rods** first. These act as mechanical amplifiers or indicators for small rotational movements of the wrist: move your hand a little, and the rod moves a lot, in much the same way as the handlebars do for steering a bicycle.

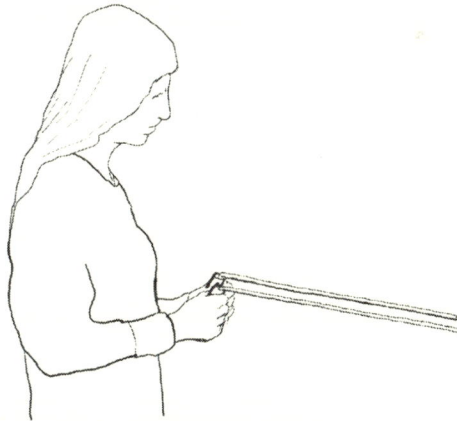

Holding angle-rods

They're typically made out of fencing wire or an unravelled coat-hanger, bent into an L-shape. Pretty much anything goes – we've seen people use folding radio-aerials, or metal 'blades' custom-made by a blacksmith – but the *mechanical* criteria for angle-rods are that:

- the vertical shaft turns freely in your hand – so it can move smoothly 'by itself'
- the horizontal arm is long enough to break 'starting friction' without being so long as to be a nuisance
- the horizontal arm is reasonably straight – so you can see where it's pointing
- there's a tight right-angle between vertical shaft and horizontal pointer – so, again, it can turn freely
- the material is light enough to hold and to turn freely, but heavy enough to not get caught in the wind

Medium-gauge fencing-wire with a horizontal arm of around twelve to eighteen inches (30-50cm) and a vertical shaft of around three to six inches (8-15cm) will satisfy those criteria well. It can also be helpful to use handles or sleeves for the vertical shaft, perhaps made from wood or cotton-reels or a discarded ball-point pen, but they're not essential.

Some people use only a single rod: it works well as a pointer to follow a direction. But paired rods give more choice of expression – cross-over, pointer, parallel and so on – so we'll use that in what follows.

In practical use of the rods, we'll see wide variations in personal style; but remember that the role of the rods is to act as amplifiers for small movements of the wrists. So the *mechanical* criteria here are that:

- the horizontal arm needs to be able to swing freely from side to side – hence handles are useful, but not required
- the horizontal arm needs to be just below a horizontal level – if it's too low there won't much amplification, if it's too high it'll be too unstable
- the wrist needs to be able to rotate freely – the best posture for this is with your arms about body-width apart at waist-height, with the forearms roughly level with the horizontal

So, for example, we'll often see people holding the rods with hands close together, clamped tight against the chest; but in practice it's perhaps not a good idea. It might feel safer, perhaps, or more controlled, but for purely mechanical reasons, holding the rods in that way will make it harder to get good results. Keep things simple, keep it free and easy, to give quality a chance to come through.

The classic angle-rods response is the cross-over – also known as 'X marks the spot'. But we really need to develop a full *vocabulary* of responses, to give us a broader ranger of pointers to interpretations. Some common examples include:

- cross-over – the point where the rods cross is the location
- squint (rods leaning slightly towards each other) – often used as active-neutral, such as when tracking along a line
- double-point (both rods pointing to one side) – in tracking, line bends in the direction shown by the rods
- single-point (one rod continues to point forward, the other points outward or across) – in tracking, typically implies a junction, or another line crossing at a different level
- splay (both rods pointing in opposite directions) – T-junction on a line, or dead-end
- spin (one or both rods spinning) – variously interpreted as a 'blind spring' (water moving up or down), or some kind of 'energy node'
- null (both rods exactly parallel, accompanied by a 'nothing' feel) – passive-neutral, often implies 'lost it', lost the connection

As for what this *means*? Well, more on that in a moment. First, though, the other most common instrument, the **pendulum**.

Holding a pendulum

This is a small weight suspended below the fingers, so that, again, a small side-to-side movement of your hand is made more visible. The mechanical criteria are as follows:

- the closer the weight is to symmetrical in shape, the more stable and predictable in response
- a point at the base of the weight makes it easier to see what's going on
- the string-length should be constant – hence holding the string between finger and thumb is more reliable than draping it over a finger
- the string-length determines period of swing, and should ideally match the natural resonance of the hand- and arm-muscles – hence a typical length of around one to three inches (3-8cm)
- the weight needs to be light enough to respond quickly, but heavy enough to not be blown around by the wind

From the above, the 'best' pendulum is a spherical shape with a point, such as smallish version of a traditional brass builder's plumb-bob; use a lighter one for indoor work, a heavier one on site. In principle, though, you can use whatever you like – we've seen people use anything from a tiny crystal to a wooden toy-soldier, from a four-pound pottery gnome to a used teabag – but note that it does tend to get harder to use the further you go from those mechanical criteria.

There's also one mechanical criterion about usage, to do with starting-inertia. Some people use a 'static neutral' – in other words the pendulum indicates neutral when it's completely still. The problem with that is that it takes time for the pendulum to 'wake up', in a mechanical sense – which means that you may have already moved past a point by the time there's any visible response on the pendulum. So we usually recommend a 'dynamic neutral', where a small forward-and-back movement indicates neutral, because the pendulum can 'wake up' much more quickly.

Many people use opposite rotations to distinguish between positive and negative responses to questions – for example, clockwise means 'Yes', counter-clockwise means 'No'. As with the angle-rods, though, it's useful to build a broader vocabulary of responses, including:

- positive and negative – clockwise and counter-clockwise, as above, are typically used for this

- pointer – typically, the angle of swing indicates direction
- 'idiot' response, as 'unask the question', because the context is such that neither 'Yes' nor 'No' would make sense – a side-to-side swing is often used for this
- null, the 'lost it' response – a dead stop is often used to indicate this, confirmed by a 'nothing' feel

Whatever the instrument we use, the trick is that it should *feel* as if it's moving all by itself. Just remember that it isn't: it's the hands that are actually doing it.

As for *why* the hands are moving, and what it all means – well, it's just coincidence, really... And to make sense of *that*, we need to look a little more closely at 'coincidence'.

It's all coincidence

Dowsing is all about finding a coincidence between what you're looking for, and where you are. The complication is that the ways we define what we're looking for, and sometimes even where we are, may well be imaginary, in the sense we create some kind of image of them to work with. So when someone dismisses dowsing as "entirely coincidence and mostly imaginary", we might have to sort-of agree with them, because it is indeed entirely coincide-ence and mostly image-inary.

Let's put that in more practical terms:

- you need some way to define what you're looking for
- you need some way to identify where you are
- you need some way to recognise the coincide-ence between them

To define what you're looking for, the classic method is to carry a sample or 'witness' – a small bottle of water, perhaps, or a chunk of copper wire or drain-pipe or Roman tile or whatever the target might be. It's easy, it's obvious, it's tangible, and it makes sense; it's certainly the best approach to use when you first start dowsing. Yet oddly it's clear that this physical sample isn't actually required, in the way that it would be for a machine-based sensor. In fact there's one well-known commercial set of dowsing-rods, used by maintenance crews on councils across the country, whose manual insists that whatever sample is held will be what is *not* found – so you find a clay drainage-pipe, for example, by *not* getting a response with a clay sample. Other people will use a photograph or a word or symbol as the ' sample' – it's often done that way in healing-related dowsing, for example. And for so-called 'energy dowsing', there's no physical sample that we *can* carry: instead, we have to use some kind of imagined pattern or symbol, or look for an identifiable 'signature'-pattern of responses.

The same applies to identifying the location. The simple way is to walk around, so that the location called 'where I am' is literally wherever I am – the leading edge of the leading foot is a useful marker for this. But again, this isn't an absolute restriction: we can instead *imagine* 'where I am', on a map, a drawing, an abstract diagram or the like – hence map-dowsing and so on. It gets harder, and potentially less reliable, the further we move away from the physical realm: but there's nothing to stop us doing so.

A classic example of this is what's known as the Bishop's Rule, a depth-finding technique that's been used by water-diviners for well over a century. We start off by finding water in our usual way, with a water-sample, or a colour-coded disc, or whatever. Typically, the best spot is going to be where two water-lines cross, or spiral upward in what's known as a 'blind spring'. We mark that point. We then walk *away* from that spot, this time dowsing for the depth of the water there. At some point there should be another response. We then apply the Bishop's Rule, which asserts that distance out is distance down: the distance away from the water-line is the depth.

We identify a 'meaningful coincidence' from the instrument's responses: the rods cross, the pendulum swings in a circle, and so on. The point is that *we* decide beforehand what will be meaningful, and what will not – much like tuning a radio to separate out 'signal' (the information we want) from 'noise' (which is everything else).

No-one knows how any of this 'really works': it just does. (Or at least, with practice it does!) What we *do* know is that belief seems to play an important part. So here we run up against Gooch's Paradox: things not only have to be seen to be believed, but often also have to believed to be seen. If we don't believe that dowsing can work, we're right – it doesn't work. It won't work well if we don't pay attention to what we're thinking; and it also often won't work if we try too hard. Getting the balance right around that paradox is one of the trickiest parts of the skill of dowsing...

One of the other points that's known about dowsing is that it's similar to our other kinds of physiological perception. This differs from pure physical sensing – such as with metal-detector, for example – in that what we perceive is always an *interpretation*, not the thing itself; and whilst it's good at identifying edges or other kinds of sharp change, it's not so good with continuities or with subtle change. To give an everyday example, our eyes are very good at noticing when something flicks past in a second or so, but are not so good at spotting changes that take place over minutes or more; and when given something that is completely continuous – such as in the 'white-out' of a blizzard – most people will start to hallucinate quite quickly, as the eyes try to create edges where none exist at all. The same is true in dowsing. What we perceive *seems* to be made up of edges, but that isn't necessarily what's 'really there' – it's just the way we perceive it.

So whilst may we talk about 'water lines' or 'underground streams', for example, what's actually down there below is unlikely to be the subterranean equivalent of a pretty babbling brook. If we dig down, what we're more likely to find is a band of seepage through small cracks and fissures, perhaps without even a clearly-defined cut-off between 'stream' and dry rock. But we'll *perceive* this as a distinct line, centred on the mid-point of the seepage, perhaps with an apparent width indicating the amount of flow. In other words, what we perceive is always going to be in part 'imaginary', because of the way that perception creates these pre-interpretive overlays. The same especially applies to 'energy lines' and the like: there's probably no direct equivalence to any-thing physical, but we *perceive* them as if they're physical lines. We do need to remember, though, that they're technically 'image-inary' – with everything that that implies in terms of conceptual quality. More on this later.

What's the need?

There's also what we might call 'aspirational quality', or 'ethical quality', in that *need* seems to be a factor in determining what works and what doesn't. Again, we don't know why, but it's a common experience that results tend to be more reliable if there's a genuine need – and especially a need on behalf of others rather than for ourselves.

Many dowsers use a checklist for need, which they use before starting any work on-site:

- *Can I?* – am I capable of doing the work? do I have the required skill and experience?
- *May I?* – do I have both the need and the permission of the place or context to do the work?
- *Am I ready?* – am I in the right physical and mental state to do the work?

If any of the answers is 'No', we should stop work straight away – otherwise the results are all but guaranteed to be unreliable.

This 'equation of need' also seems to be one reason why scientific-style 'tests' of dowsing tend to fail, or at least give ambiguous results. Members of the Skeptics Society and the like will point to such problems as 'proof' that dowsing 'cannot work', but in fact it's an inherent fault in science, not in the dowsing. To make sense in scientific terms, we need to be able to repeat conditions exactly, and only vary one parameter at a time. But if *need* is part of the overall equation, we have no repeatable controls for the 'need' factor, and hence no way to conduct a meaningful test. Which is a problem.

Yet it's only a problem if we depend on science for our belief. Instead, we can take a *technology* view, concerning ourselves not with 'how it works', but 'how it can be worked'. The laws of science, it seems can never be broken, so statistically we should end up with its predicted nothing-much-ness. But whilst the 'laws of science' can't be broken as such, inverse-Murphy shows us that, under the right conditions, they *can* be bent, locally, and some-times a lot – which gives us the gap in which we can do our work. We just need to remember that whenever we do so, it's Murphy that's in charge here – with everything that *that* implies, too!

A more subtle concern around 'need' in dowsing relates to its nature as a skill. The process of developing a new skill – *any* skill, that is, not just dowsing – will always bring up some personal challenges around commitment to the skill itself. To get through those challenges, we have to find some way to access our own *passion* for the skill – a drive to improve, no matter what it takes. If we can't find that burning 'inner need', our skills – and the quality of our results – may well fade away to nothing.

This applies at every stage of the process, but particularly so at that bleak point known as 'the dark night of the soul'. To under-stand this better, and what to do about it, we need to go round the bend a bit – by taking a brief detour through the labyrinthine process of learning.

Round the bend

The usual view of skills-development is that it's a linear process: we gain a steady increase in ability, each layer of training building upon those before. That seems obvious enough, yet in practice it doesn't describe the difficulties, the uncertainties, the common feeling of 'one step forward, two steps back', that are so often experienced in skills-development, and which make the development of any new skill so challenging. It's also far more than mere training: it's *the education of experience*, literally 'out-leading' that experience from within the inner depths of each person.

The 'skills-labyrinth' provides a precise metaphor that deals with these issues, in a way that's common to every skill – so it makes the learning of *any* skill an easier, less stressful experience. It uses the classic single-path maze – found in many cultures around the world – to model the various stages in the *personal* process of learning new skills.

8: Mastery
7: Meditation
6: Mind
5: Communication
4: Caring
3: Control
2: Self
1: Survival

"Beginner's Luck"

"Dark Night of the Soul"

The skills-labyrinth

The classic labyrinth pattern is a kind of maze, but with only a single twisted path. There are no choices, no branches, no junctions – so as long as we can keep going, we will eventually get to the centre. Yet with all skills, reaching that central goal – the personal mastery of some aspect of the skill – can take a *lot* longer than we'd expect: and there are plenty of opportunities to get lost along the way...

17

The most useful version for this has seven distinct sections, in what would seem to be a linear order: survival, self, control, caring, communication, mind, meditation, mastery. But that's not the sequence in which we experience them...

We start with 'beginner's luck', the classic one-weekend-workshop 'success' where we succeed *because* we don't know what we're doing. There's then a choice: either run away from the challenge – an all too common characteristic of the dilettante New Age mindset – or dive into the depths of the skill itself. If we do keep going, we move straight into 'control' – the limited sort-of-mastery that we can attain through training. But to go deeper, we have to go outward, to look at 'self', our own involvement in the skill; and then outward again, to the long, slow, painful and often barely-productive 'survival' stage – practice, practice, practice, often without much apparent point.

At the end of that 'survival' section is the worst point of all, where many people give up and abandon the skill forever. Traditionally known as 'the dark night of the soul' – and the exact opposite of the exuberance of 'beginner's luck' – it's often experienced the day before the exam, or the first live demonstration on-site, or some other crucial challenge. There *is* a way through that bleak stage: caring – a commitment to the self and to the skill itself, as much as caring in general – is the essential attribute that helps this happen. From that moment on, the skills learned so far are never lost – although as the model shows, there are a few more twists and turns to go before true mastery can be achieved!

The labyrinth model is fractal, or 'self-similar', in that it applies as much within each stage of skills-development as to the overall skill. As we'll see later, in the section on *Lost in the learning labyrinth* (p.87), it illustrates several common mistakes, such as the tendency to cling on to the brief success of 'beginner's luck'. (Playing New Age dilettante is fun, of course, but nothing actually improves...) It shows how interactions between people at different stages of a skill will contribute to confusions and mistakes; it also helps explain why reliability and proficiency *necessarily* go down during some stages of development. And by showing that the 'dark night of the soul' is an inherent part of the process, it helps to reduce the risk that people will abandon their development of skill at the moment before success – at what would be great cost to themselves and their self-esteem.

Developing our *skill* in dowsing is the only way we'll improve the *quality* of our dowsing. In turn, though, we also need to be able to identify what quality actually *is* – and in particular, the key distinctions between objective and subjective quality that underpin quality as a whole. That question of quality is what we need to look at next.

A QUESTION OF QUALITY

Objective quality

What *is* quality? In the objective world, such as in manufacturing and production-management, they have a definite answer to that question: quality is a kind of *truth*. Quality is at its best when the end-product matches exactly to some predefined standard – a reference-pattern, a rule-book, a design-specification or the like.

So there's a whole industry built up around 'quality' in the business context. For straightforward commercial reasons, there's a great deal of sense in amongst those impenetrable acronyms such as ISO-9000, Six Sigma, TQM and the rest – so if you're interested in improving quality in general, you'll find it worth exploring the reference-sites such as Wikipedia. There's also a useful model called Cynefin, which partitions decision-making into four distinct domains: known, knowable, complex, and chaotic.

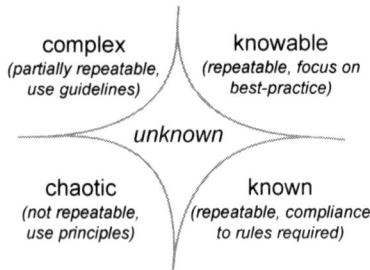

complex
*(partially repeatable,
use guidelines)*

knowable
*(repeatable, focus on
best-practice)*

unknown

chaotic
*(not repeatable,
use principles)*

known
*(repeatable, compliance
to rules required)*

Cynefin decision-making styles

In principle at least, objective quality is the same for everyone. It expects its world to be *known* – based on clear rules, clear patterns of cause and effect. There are procedures, work-instructions, the fast-food franchise handbook that describes 'the one right way' to mop the floor. Deviation from the standard is anathema: there's no time or tolerance for anything more than training, no place for skill or personal difference. Following the rules assures a quality result; and the rules alone will suffice.

When the world becomes too complicated for that, we move on to analysis, the domain of the *knowable*. But there's still always an assumption of certainty and control, that there will always be some true standard against which quality can be confirmed. So it's here that we'll find a focus on facts, on statistical analysis of results; and here too we'll see a detailed exploration of 'best practice' in every possible work-context.

Unlike the procedure-manuals, the idea of best-practice does at least acknowledge that the world can be different in different places and for different people. It doesn't assume there's only one 'right way to do it': instead, it describes what's been known to work well elsewhere, and provide some guidance as to how to adapt it to the local conditions. Which is a lot more helpful, really.

But it still doesn't make much allowance for uncertainty, or the kind of 'one-off' contexts which we find ourselves dealing with so often in dowsing. For those, we need to consider more than just objective quality: we also need to understand and maintain an appropriate balance with the subjective side of quality.

Subjective quality

As soon as we introduce skill – in fact as soon as we introduce a real person – there has to be a subjective side to quality. What's true for me – my understanding of what is quality, and what is not - may well not be true for you, and vice versa. Quality exists, quality is real, but we can't define what it *is*: there's no fixed standard against which to measure.

Instead of 'truth', the measure of quality here is *value* – what it means, how it feels, in a personal sense. There is still a kind of truth, though, that comes from respect for the material, the context itself, as typified in Michelangelo's comment about 'to free the sculpture from within the stone'.

There's also a need for commitment to the skill 'for its own sake'. Good workmanship shows good quality, clear evidence of what Robert Pirsig, in his classic *Zen and the Art of Motorcycle Maintenance*, described as 'gumption'. We may not be able to define beforehand what the end-result will be, yet we have a clear idea of what it would look like – and even more of what it won't. The end-result may be finely-polished, perhaps, the work of months or years, or it may be rough-hewn, simple, assembled in a matter of moments; yet the quality – or lack of it – will usually be evident for all to see, or feel. In that sense, qualitative value both has and is its own truth.

Objective quality expects its world to be certain, to be repeatable, and repeatable by anyone. Subjective quality doesn't: instead, it accepts that its world is acausal, complex, chaotic – in a word, *messy*. There may well be some kind of 'self-similarity', but nothing is ever quite the same. Yet even if there are no certainties, no fixed rules to follow, quality still exists: we don't simply throw our hands up in the air and say "anything goes". In the complex domain, where things still have a semblance of repeatability, we can hold to proven guidelines and 'rules of thumb'; and in the chaotic domain, where things aren't repeatable at all, we turn to principles that have stood the test of time – such as an awareness of the different layers in the skills-labyrinth. It works.

What also works is a different kind of sharing. Where the complicated, 'knowable' end of objective quality relies on best-practice, those who deal with worlds that are inherently uncertain – maintenance engineers, for example – will turn to '*worst*-practice', stories about what didn't work, and the experiments they went through to fix it. There's also more emphasis on 'communities of practice', to help that sharing of stories, and assist newcomers in making sense of what's going on in their personal quest for quality.

Quality in practice

So what does all of this mean for the disciplines of dowsing, and for other subjective skills?

The first answer is that all of the above applies: we're always dealing with both kinds of quality, objective and subjective. Because it's a skill, subjective quality will tend to come to the fore; but the moment we want to *do* anything with our results, we'd better be sure that the objective facts are there too.

So how do we do that? One tactic is to use the same layered approach as in business quality-management:

- *principles* – the overall 'guiding star' for all of the work
- *policies* – 'approaches', decisions about how we approach changes to the work
- *procedures* – 'mechanics', decisions about how we think about the work, how we change what we do and how we do it
- *work-instructions* – 'methods', decisions about how we do the work.

Our starting point is the 'product' of the work – which in the case of dowsing is an *opinion*, about a desired or identified coincidence of what is looked for and where we are. We then use those opinions as appropriate, according to the context, but those opinions or judgements are at the core of what we do.

Vision / Principles

Policy

Procedure

Work-Instruction

Layers of quality-management

In practice, we run the quality-management sequence backwards. We start from the work-instructions – for which the dowsing equivalents are things like 'hold the rods this way', 'mark your location this way', 'use this kind of sample for this purpose', and so on. That gives us something repeatable, a known reference-point, which will be drawn from some kind of best-practice – either from someone else, or our own.

> The checklist 'Can I? May I? Am I ready?', which many dowsers use before starting work, is a good example of a work-instruction: it's a defined series of steps, which leads to a decision – in this case, to work, or to not work.

When that work-instruction doesn't fit any more, or doesn't seem to work well, we move upward to the procedure, to create a new work-instruction. This is where we need that information about mechanical criteria for the instrument; likewise the more subtle 'mechanics' about thinking-processes and the like. We use these to assess the context, and guide a design for another way of working.

> A simple example: our usual work-instruction for archaeological sites is to use lightweight rods, but they don't work well in windy conditions. Going up to the procedure gets us thinking about mechanical criteria: so for this site we decide to use heavier rods, tilt the rods down slightly – to reduce over-sensitivity – and rest the thumbs lightly on the bend to apply a bit of damping to the movement.

When the context changes so much that this doesn't work either, the standard says that we need to move upward again to policy. In a dowsing sense, this is where we shift from 'objective' to subjective: not so much about what we *do*, as the way in which we *approach* what we do, how we make our decisions, and so on.

In much of dowsing work we'll use beliefs as tools – in the Bishop's Rule, for example, we change from the belief that the rods will cross over water, to a belief that they will cross at a point the same distance out from mark-point to the depth down to the water. In effect, the 'procedure' here is the way we apply Gooch's Paradox: things have to believed to be seen, so we *choose* to change belief according to the context.

To do this, we also need some way to keep track at each moment of what we're believing, what we're choosing to believe, whether there's any difference, and whether the choice of belief is working. Kind of mind-bending, in an all too literal sense!

The 'policy' here is that we need all of these things, in a way that works well for us, together with a kind of 'watching of the watcher'. This suggests a set of requirements – a procedure – for some form of active meditation, and where and when and why. In turn, the derived work-instructions identify the specific form of meditation we choose to use, how to use it, and so on.

When appropriate care in all of this still doesn't give us the results we need, we move all the way up to vision and principle – the final 'guiding stars' for everything we do. This is where that 'equation of need' comes in, for example: hence one useful principle in dowsing is a cultivated selflessness – "take of the fruit for others, or forebear".

Yet this also takes us back full circle, because the ultimate root of dowsing is in precision of *feeling*. What exactly do we feel, at each place, at each moment, at each potential co-incidence? The instrument's responses may be the only visible part of what we do; yet the instrument itself is just a way to externalise feelings - angle-rods as crutches for a limping intuition, if you like.

So the 'guiding stars' for quality in dowsing are those four principles we saw earlier:

- precision in *sensing*
- precision in *identifying locations* and facts
- precision in *deriving meaning* from coincide-ence of sensing and location
- precision in *use of meaning* – which also includes ethics.

Ultimately, what *use* is it? How do we identify quality in that use? For each of these, the answer lies in discipline – the four disciplines of the disciplined dowser.

THE DISCIPLINED DOWSER

If an emphasis on quality is bad enough, talking about discipline may well sound worse. Memories of primary-school, of standing in the corner, "not enough discipline" and all that...

Don't worry – it's not like that! (Well, maybe a *little* bit, we could say with a grin... But at least here we do explain what discipline *is*, why it's a useful habit to develop – for *your* benefit, that is – and how to develop it. Which is more than they gave you at school, we'd guess?)

> Some of what follows may seem a bit abstract at first: but once again, don't worry! It'll make more sense when we go into practice in more detail over the next few chapters.
>
> This kind of 'theory stuff' does provide a useful overview, though we'll admit it can sometimes seem a distraction when you already have a known way of working – a 'work-instruction' – and whilst you're doing the work itself. Where it really comes into its own is when you need to re-think what you're doing and how you're doing it – in other words, when you have to move up to the 'procedure' level and above. If you don't have some consistent theoretical frame to work with at those levels, you can write yourself into a corner very quickly indeed – as you'll see in the *Seven sins of dubious discipline* (p.65).
>
> In short, yes, perhaps it might feel a bit confusing now, especially if you're itching to get back to practice – but trust us, you'll find that paying attention to this stuff at this point will turn out to be *really* valuable later on.

In itself, there's nothing difficult in discipline. It's very simple: it's about developing a habit to *plan* and prepare for the work we intend to do; to notice what we *do*, and what we're thinking whilst we're doing it; to *check* whether these are in accord with what we've chosen to do; and *take action* as appropriate to change any of these if there are any concerns with quality.

> In the business world this is known as the Total Quality Management cycle: Plan; Do; Check; Act.
>
> Plan ↗ ↘ Do
>
> Act ↖ ↙ Check
>
> *Total Quality Management cycle*

> In meditation, too, we *prepare* for the practice; *do* the practice; review and re-assess to *check* the practice; and *act* to change the practice where needed.
>
> Different contexts, but the overall discipline – and the overall need for discipline – is much the same everywhere.

What complicates it a little in dowsing is that there are four distinct strands or modes or 'disciplines' that we need to keep track of within the overall discipline. We need to understand what these modes are, what we can and can't do within each, and how and when and why to switch between them.

Remember our earlier summary of dowsing, that it's about *sensing* at an *identifiable location* to derive information that's *meaningful* and *useful*. The information comes from our sensing of a co-incidence between what we're looking for and where we are, and it may be a quality (a direction, a 'feel') or a quantity (a number, a count, or a simple yes-or-no). So the four disciplines are these:

- sensing – the dowser as *artist*
- define what we're looking for, identify where we are – the dowser as *scientist*
- derive meaning – the dowser as *mystic*
- derive usefulness – the dowser as *magician*

> If the word 'magician' seems uncomfortable, call it 'technologist' instead – the two terms are actually the same, as we'll explain later. But then some people might be even more uncomfortable about describing themselves as 'technologists', too… Oh well – it's just a label, anyway!

As for why we emphasise just these four modes, it's probably simplest to explain with a diagram:

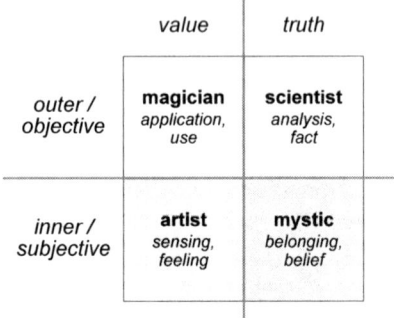

	value	truth
outer / objective	**magician** *application, use*	**scientist** *analysis, fact*
inner / subjective	**artist** *sensing, feeling*	**mystic** *belonging, belief*

The four disciplines

You'll see that there's a strong correlation between this and the Cynefin model we showed earlier (see p.20). There's also another view of the same frame in Tom's book *Inventing Reality: towards a magical technology*, in which the four modes are four different ways of working in a swamp: keep moving fast (the Artist), climb up a pole for overview (the Mystic), build a solid platform (the Scientist), or spread your weight on swamp-shoes (the Magician).

In effect, this is a not-quite-arbitrary split of the world of dowsing work across two dimensions:

- *subjective* ↔ *objective*, or personal ↔ shared / common
- *value* ↔ *truth*, or qualitative ↔ quantitative

This gives us four distinct modes: subjective value, subjective truth, objective truth, objective value. Each mode or discipline provides its own distinctive view into the whole, and also has distinct tactics that we would use within that mode – though *only* within that mode.

So for example, the discipline that we're calling 'dowser as artist' is all about subjective value, those aspects of dowsing that are strictly personal, that belong to self alone – about the ways we sense and experience our various impressions of the site and its context. When we place our focus on that 'artist' mode, we pay careful attention to what we feel at each place, how we feel, what we sense, how we could portray what we sense, and so on, as well as the responses of any dowsing-instrument we might be using at the time.

What we *don't* allow when we're in that Artist mode is any intrusion from beliefs and expectations (from the Mystic, subjective truth), from matters of measurement and the like (the Scientist, objective truth), or from concerns about the end-purpose (the Magician, objective value). Each of those other modes is certainly relevant, and we need to pay our full attention to them all within the dowsing practice – *but not at the same time.*

At each moment, we're in just *one* mode, using just *one* type of discipline; and to make sense of the whole, we move between the modes, cleanly, consciously, explicitly, moment by moment. There are paths between modes that are mutually supportive, such as Artist → Magician → Scientist → Mystic, the dowser's equivalent of the classic sequence 'idea → hypothesis → theory → law' that's so important in the sciences. Each mode is distinct, and some can be mutually antagonistic, particularly Artist ↔ Scientist, or Mystic ↔ Magician. And we also need to take care not to get stuck in one or two preferred modes, but maintain a balance between them all. So there's also an implied fifth discipline about the process of switching disciplines – an *integration* that unites all these different views into the single overall discipline of dowsing.

It's likely, then, that the single most important factor for quality in dowsing is understanding which mode we're in at any given time, and working appropriately to match the constraints of that mode. And if our work is to be meaningful and useful to others, we also need to know how to present our results in ways that are appropriate to the respective mode: we *don't* present ideas as facts, or vice versa.

So let's look at each of these disciplines in more detail.

THE DOWSER AS ARTIST

Principles…

At its root, dowsing depends on precision of *sensing*. The rod moves because the hand moves; and the hand moves because we sense something.

And like an artist, a craftsman at work, there's an emphasis here on subtleties of feeling, on 'experiences' – "what do I *feel*?"

Feelings and sensing are also part of how we build relationship with place. We *respond* to the place – and often find that it in turn will respond to us, if we let it do so.

Each feeling is whatever happens by within that fleeting moment. The process of thinking, of analysis, tends to get in the way here, as precision tends to fall apart if any response is too 'considered'. Instead, there's a need to let go into the flow, to "just *be*, man…". So the key tactic here, as suggested by the Cynefin model, is 'act / sense / respond': we *do* something – almost anything, really – so as to create a space in which sensing can occur, which in turn provides the response we see on the instrument or in some other way.

It's not about truth here: the nearest we get to 'truth' would be a phrase like "I serve the truth of the work itself". The sensings and feelings have their own truth, if you like.

Yet whatever we experience is subjective, is ours alone. In itself, its value is ours alone, too. Even though it's surprising how often a feeling will parallel those experienced by others in the same place, anything we may experience does not *necessarily* have any meaning for anyone else – or even mean anything at all. It just *is*.

So the one real problem with this mode is that, by itself, it doesn't *do* anything: it's about experiencing, feeling, but *only* about feeling, without any particular connection to anything else. To make any sense at all here, we have to switch briefly into some

29

other mode – but without losing connection with that inner space from which we do the sensing. Can be a bit tricky, that…

The expression of the feeling is the anchor for that feeling – literally 'real-ises' the feeling. Obviously, in dowsing, the usual and most evident expression for each feeling or sensing will be in the instrument's response – the movements of the rods, the gyrations of the pendulum, and so on. We may find, though, that some feelings and sensings may be better expressed in other forms: in drawings or paintings, perhaps, or even in poetry – whatever the Muses may require of us, really.

The dowser as artist… feeling, sensing, listening, *being*.

…and practice

The role of the Artist mode is to *notice*, to pay attention.

The Artist manages that which is inherently *chaotic* – unique, one-off, with no apparent connection to anything else.

The Artist responds to the context through a sense of *inner value*, whatever feels right in the moment, with a decision-sequence of act → sense → respond.

You'll need to use the Artist discipline when:

- you need to know what you're sensing or feeling
- you're on a site for the first time
- you want to start afresh, in any sense
- when the context is 'one-off' or inherently uncertain

You'll know you're in the Artist mode when:

- there's a response on the dowsing-instrument – especially if the instrument responds in an unexpected way
- a 'side-feeling' comes through (see below)
- there's an urge to portray what's going on, a desire to create as a way to commit to something memory
- there's a general sense of childlike wonder, of exuberance, energy, excitement, enthusiasm, 'in-the-moment-ness'

Rules that apply in the Artist discipline include:

- "anything goes" – there is no 'right' or 'wrong', the feeling or response is what it is
- the response exists only in the moment – if you wait around, or try to hold onto it, it'll be gone

- the response needs some form of expression if it is to be 'realised', made real
- the response is personal – it does not necessarily mean anything to anyone else, or 'mean' anything at all – it just *is*

Warning-signs of dubious Artist discipline include:

- "this means...", "this proves..." *[blurring Artist with Scientist or Mystic]*
- "this has no purpose...", "this feeling gets in the way..." *[blurring Artist with Magician or Mystic]*
- "I should not feel this...", "I ought to feel...", "this is not what I want to feel..." *[blurring Artist with Mystic, or just overdose of ego]*
- "the feeling I had here last time was..." *[blurring Artist with Scientist]*

To bridge across to the Mystic, focus on:

- what are my thoughts or beliefs before, whilst and after I feel this?
- to what does this feeling belong?
- what does this feeling tell me about my relationship with the place? does it feel 'right to be here', or warning of 'wrong to be here' or suchlike?

To bridge across to the Magician, focus on:

- how can I use this?
- how can I express this?
- in what forms put a 'handle' on this to commit it to memory? – taste, sound, take a photograph, whatever

To bridge across to the Scientist (hardest), focus on:

- where is this happening?
- when is this happening?
- what is the context when this happens?
- has this feeling happened before at this place, this time, this context?
- what else is happening when I sense this?

In this mode, dowsing is all about being, exploring feelings and ideas and experiences in a different way. Everything happens in the moment; the moment *is* the happening. Questions about the purpose or use of dowsing, or how it works, or even whether it works at all, have no real relevance here: it all just *is*.

So in this context the purest form of dowsing would be what's called 'deviceless dowsing' – no divining-rod or pendulum or other external instrument, but instead just sensing out the body's own moment-by-moment responses to place.

> Used as a conventional dowsing-technique, deviceless dowsing makes use of the fact that many people have their own natural responses to underground water and the like. For example, one of Tom's students used to hiccup every time she went over water – quite embarrassing at times, as her head jerked up and down like an ostrich when she was tracking along a water-line.
>
> For most of us, fortunately, that natural response is usually a bit more subtle, though can also take a bit more awareness to notice within ourselves. One suggestion to try here would be that many people find that rubbing index-finger and thumb together lightly can work well for this: the digits tend to 'stick' to indicate a response, and move smoothly past each other as the 'neutral'.
>
> When you do identify what works for you, and learn to use it as your 'instrument', deviceless dowsing can be very useful indeed – especially in public places, where overt dowsing with rods or pendulum will usually attract all too much unwanted attention!

On its own, the Artist mode isn't much use – isn't even *about* 'use', in fact. But where it *is* very useful indeed is in what we describe as the 'side-feelings' that come up whilst working. For the main process in dowsing, we set up some kind of belief that the instrument will give us something from its regular vocabulary of responses, to indicate 'yes' or 'no' or the like. We use the Mystic mode to maintain focus on that belief. But we also leave a small space for other hints and feelings to come through, to point out when we need to look a little wider than a simplistic 'yes/no'. It may point out a direction, perhaps, or suggest there's something else we need to know about – for example, when there's a power-cable that crosses where our water-divining has shown us an otherwise preferred spot to dig down for water... Whatever it may be, we *need* to leave space for those side-feelings to come through.

> In some of our recent archaeography work at ancient sites, we've been experimenting with a form of deviceless dowsing which keeps the focus almost exclusively on these side-feelings.
>
> We usually work as a pair, to provide some degree of cross-reference and objectivity, and to simplify the recording process. Walking around the boundaries of the site, or in a regular pattern across it, we note down what feelings and impressions and body-sensations come up – noting in particular where they're the same for both of us, and where they're different. We then use a hiker's GPS (Global Positioning

System) unit to keep track of location, with the date, time and position of each sensing recorded on the GPS as a 'waypoint'.

This automatically builds up a map of sensings and their locations, which we can also plot onto a conventional map or site-plan. Given the current limitations of GPS technology, it's not as precise as proper dowsing – it's only accurate to two or three paces at best – but still enough to derive interesting information to correlate with dowsing-results or conventional archaeology reports. More later, anyway, in the section on fieldwork (see p.112) and in some of the 'worked examples' (see p.119).

From the Mystic mode's perspective, dowsing is a kind of meditation which keeps the focus on the instrument; but the Artist adds its own side-meditation to notice what *else* happens whilst we do so. In *Zen and the Art of Motorcycle Maintenance*, Robert Pirsig describes this process as 'fishing for facts': we dangle a line over the side, so to speak, and see what facts come by to take a bite. They may not be useful straight off, but it's always worthwhile paying attention: as Pirsig put it, sometimes these facts will have friends, and they bring *their* friends along too – and somewhere in amongst them will be ones that we really need to know!

It's useful, too, to take what's known as a Fortean approach to this. In the Artist mode, everything we experience simply *is* – it need not have any connection with anything else at all. So we record it as best we can, exactly 'as-is', *without* any attempt at interpretation. Interpretation of events belongs in another mode entirely, usually the Scientist or the Mystic; we can do it later if we want, but mixing modes at the same time is all but guaranteed to ruin the quality of work. We'll come back to this later when we look at the practical problems of the Reality Risk (see p.82).

One of the harder aspects of the Artist is to find an appropriate way to express the sensings. The impressions are fleeting, and exist only in the moment; yet it takes *time* to record or express them. So a significant part of the discipline is to hold on to the impressions without holding on, so to speak. In this, Pirsig's 'friends' are our main allies: the sensings themselves evaporate within moments, but they can bring something else with them that's enough for us to embody as a slightly longer-lived memory. Later, we can translate that memory and its associated feelings into some form of expression – painting, drawing, writing, poetry, dance, music, or whatever else the Muses might suggest. Yet it can often be extraordinarily hard to express this in a way which feels like it does describe the original sensing…

33

Liz spent a couple of decades as a professional illustrator for archaeology, doing painstaking pen-and-ink drawings of finds from Neolithic, Bronze Age, Iron Age and Roman sites. Yet in some ways there's not that much of the Artist there – it's more somewhere between the Scientist and the Magician, precise measurement interpreted to a practical use, even if primarily an academic one.

So for some years now she's moved over more into archaeography – a formal discipline that forms a bridge between archaeology, art and culture. These days her main medium is oil-paint on canvas – which might sound easier than her previous work, perhaps, but in reality it's *much* harder. Selecting out and illustrating the subtle details on a Romano-British belt-buckle does take skill and experience, but at least the object sits still on the workbench for days at a time; by contrast, capturing an emotion at a place, or an impression of fast-moving energies flowing out and round a site, is much more challenging!

For each of us, any medium we choose to express the Artist is, of necessity, a personal choice, and in part also a personal response to the context. But it's worth making a point of celebrating the Artist mode by complementing our dowsing with something – in any medium, really – that can capture and express for us that free-flowing response in the moment.

In themselves, such expressions do not necessarily 'mean' anything: that isn't their purpose. But they can *aid* interpretation of dowsing-results, and also, through what we might call crosslinks between the 'muses', help to build up a kind of holographic sense of the site as a whole – which in itself creates new information, new possibilities.

New ideas can often arise from a kind of 'total immersion', seeing groups of images as a set of multiple, overlapping views into the same context. In her archaeography work, Liz will cover an entire wall with sketches, drawings, diagrams, photographs and found objects; reviewing these as a set triggers off new cross-references and correlations, which lead to new images and new fieldwork experiments.

Archaeology dowsers might do this, for example, in creating layered diagrams of a site, with water-lines, track-lines, ground-disturbance and the like separated out into overlaid historical periods. Geopathic-stress dowsers do much the same with overlays of black-streams, Curry-grids and electromagnetic field interference patterns marked out on a house-plan. Each to their own: the point here is that the set itself is an artefact that the Artist mode can use.

And the dowsing itself can be a direct expression of the Artist. A fair number of dowsers report that they find not just water-lines and the like at 'sacred sites', but also symbolic patterns that seem to change and increase in complexity and sophistication each time they visit the site. Hamish Miller, for example, has done extensive work of this type, mapping similar-seeming patterns from different sites right around the world.

These do seem to represent and express a real personal relationship with place – though we'd recommend that it's best to take a strict Fortean approach, and stop right there, in terms of interpretation. Taking it beyond that point – such as suggesting that the changes somehow represent 'changing consciousness of place', or that any patterns we perceive indicate some fixed 'pattern of the past' – risks blurring the Artist with the Mystic or the Scientist, which can dump us straight into serious 'sins' such as the Newage Nuisance (see p.69), the Meaning Mistake (see p.72) or even the dangers of the Reality Risk (see p.82). Which would *not* be a good idea…

There's a subtlety here that's easy to miss – and missing it can cause an inexorable slide into newage or worse.

Notice again what we said above: take a strict Fortean approach, and record any earth-patterns or the like *without* interpretation. Use the Artist's attitude of "isn't it interesting…?", but unless you can then fully engage the Scientist – with all the precision that requires – *don't* make the mistake of saying "therefore this means…". The sensings we note at a place may well seem to change over time, not only for us, but for others as well; yet that does *not* mean that we have 'caused' the change – it simply *is*.

Sure, for many people – ourselves included – there's a real desire to *know* that we've created some kind of constructive change in the world. This need for subjective value in a personal sense is every bit as strong as the need for certainty and 'higher Truth' in the Mystic mode. Yet if we're not careful, there's a real vanity-trap here: the delusion of being '*the* healer of the world'.

So dowsers are at particular risk of the 'earth-healer' variant of this delusion. For example, we've seen one group build what'd be best described as a kind of ersatz religion, measuring the apparent effect of their 'world-healing' meditations and the like, by monitoring perceived patterns around a fountain in a public park. In reality, it's unlikely they measured anything more than the inflation of their own egos; and unfortunately there's no doubt at all, from Tom's painful first-hand experience with one of their sub-groups in Australia, that they often did more than harm than good at the 'earth-energies' level. And an odd, unpleasant arrogance also pervaded everything they did, with a kind of smug 'holier than thou' attitude that typified the worst of the Golden-Age Game (see p.67). Not good…

Patterns at sites are simply what and how we perceive in the Artist mode: but they're representations of personal perception, not 'fact' – and they don't *mean* anything as such. 'Meaning' comes from the Mystic and the Scientist: and there are still far too many factors, most of them still all but unknown, for us to derive any kind of meaning at all from those patterns as yet. So for now, until a *lot* more work has been done, it's best to relegate any notions of 'changes in earth-consciousness' and the like to the realm of the Artist, or perhaps the Mystic – and *don't* dupe yourself into thinking that they represent any kind of firm 'fact'. Along that latter path, There Be Dragons, or at the least some dangerously destructive delusions – You Have Been Warned!

The discipline of the Artist provides us with dowsing's means to perceive, our means to build and identify our relationship with place. Yet whatever we perceive has no meaning *in itself*: to derive meaning, or interpret meaning, we must always look elsewhere, to another mode.

Such as the Mystic, which is the discipline we'll explore next.

THE DOWSER
AS MYSTIC

Principles…

In dowsing, much of the *meaning*
that can be derived from the
instrument is predetermined by
reference to a previously-chosen belief. And in the same way,
much of the dowser's connection with place is created by a kind of
spiritual sense of belonging to and with the place.

Like a mystic, then, there's an emphasis here on the subtleties of
the inner world – "what do I *believe*? where do I *belong*?"

Driving these in turn is a deep concern for perceived *truth*: "I
believe it *because* it is true"; "I belong here *because* this is a place of
truth". Commitment to a chosen 'truth' is also the means by which
we resolve Gooch's Paradox, that in the subjective space things
not only have to be seen to be believed, but also have to be
believed to be seen.

So another key role of this mode is to create boundaries, between
true or not-true, between in or out, 'sacred' or 'profane', and so
on. These ensure that the appropriate Cynefin tactic here is 'sense
/ categorise / respond': note what seems to be going on, and
immediately place it either within or outside of the bounds of the
chosen category. The truth *itself* defines the meaning: "the rods
will *only* cross when I stand directly above water". This certainty
permits very fast responses: the catch is that in itself it has no way
to check whether the categorisation is valid, other than that sense
of certainty – 'the Law' – that comes from the chosen 'truth'.

Although the 'truth' here is actually subjective – a personal choice
– it will usually *feel* objective. "I serve a higher Truth", is the
feeling: and importantly, success *depends* on an absence of doubt
(hence the great Christian apologia, "credo quia absurdum est", "I
believe *because* it is absurd"). Doubt belongs elsewhere: any testing
of the *appropriateness* of a belief, for example, must take place only
in another mode – usually the Magician, though the Scientist and
Artist each have relevant roles for that. But here, having chosen to

believe that the rods will cross over water, for example, we then have to trust that they will do so; lack of faith – lack of belief – will almost guarantee that it can't and won't work.

Yet too much intensity of 'faith' will also get in the way: there's a fine balance needed here... Hence the practical value in dowsing of spiritual disciplines such as meditation and the like – using the movements of the instrument as a focus for the meditation, and in turn the meditation as a focus for the instrument, keeping the mind clear of any other intrusions.

> A key problem with this mode is that, on its own, it doesn't *do* anything: all it does is focus, and believe – and unlike the Scientist, its belief is beyond reason. Its 'truth' is a subjective choice, yet to work well must *feel* absolute, objective, not '*a* truth' but '*the* Truth'. Doubt and difference here are anathema, heresy, blasphemy even.
>
> So a danger here is that the necessary over-certainty and need to *belong* also create a much higher risk of becoming ensnared in the *Seven sins of dubious discipline* (p.65) – particularly the Golden-Age Game, the Newage Nuisance, the Meaning Mistake and the Possession Problem. And it's unfortunate that much so-called 'spiritual dowsing' seems all but designed to enhance those risks than reduce them...

In terms of physiology, this mode does provide the best fit to the way that perception works. Most of our senses and reflexes are best at detecting sharp edges – true/not-true, yes/no, this way not that way – and are less effective in assessing subtle gradations of tone, especially at the speed most dowsers need to work. So this mode is best expressed by the sharp changes that can be shown on a dowsing instrument: the dip and rise of a spring-rod, the quick cross-over of angle-rods, the rapid response in a pendulum's swing – a clear-cut yes or no, a clear indication of either tracking along a line or losing it. It provides a sense of *definiteness* that isn't available so strongly in any of the other modes: and that certainty is something that we *need* in dowsing practice, as long as we take care to watch for the risks.

Like the Artist, the Mystic also has its own artistic expression – though often it may take a strange symbolic form. Many dowsers report finding symbols, or something like them, in surveys around particular points. There's no doubt that these are real, in their own way: mistakes can occur, though, if we take those symbols to be 'true' in the same sense as the strict yes-or-no other responses in this mode, and treat them as objective 'fact' rather than a subjective, *personal* interaction with place.

The dowser as mystic... being, belonging, *believing*, holding fast to a higher truth.

...and practice

The role of the Mystic mode is to *focus*, and to maintain that focus.

The Mystic manages that which is inherently *known* – delving ever deeper into the meaning of a known 'universal truth'.

The Mystic responds to the context through a sense of *inner truth*, acting on a clear certainty of right and wrong, with a decision-sequence of sense → categorise → respond.

You'll need to use the Mystic discipline when:

- you define what it is you're looking for, and how the instrument should respond when you've found it
- you're keeping focus on the task whilst you're working
- you establish relationship with place before, when starting, during and whilst closing the work-session

You'll know you're in the Mystic mode when:

- there is a sense of certainty, combined with a kind of quiet calm
- there is a sense of 'connectedness' with place
- there is a subtle sense of heightened perception – background sounds may seem clearer, for example
- there's a sense of being somewhat 'outside of self', of feeling like an outside observer watching what's going on
- characteristic yet personal signals occur – for example, a perception of a slight mist around angle-rods
- there is an emphasis on the symbolic – such as expressed in ritualised actions, in checklists, and in sigils, talismans and other symbolic artefacts

Rules that apply in the Mystic discipline include:

- there is only one truth
- there is a definite boundary between true and not-true, right and wrong
- consistent focus on the one truth will provide all the answers ("we connect through that truth to higher knowledge")
- faith is the force that holds everything together – don't doubt!

Warning-signs of dubious Mystic discipline include:

- "is this the right way to...?" [*it's essential to avoid all self-doubt here, other than as a bridge to other modes*]
- "this is true for me, therefore it is true for all..." [*blurring Mystic (subjective) with Scientist (objective)*]
- "any who hold different beliefs are of lesser [or greater] worth..." [*overdose of ego, also blurring Mystic with Magician – using 'truth' for value-judgements*]
- "I am the one who causes change...", "my spirituality causes the place to change its consciousness..." [*blurring Mystic self-certainty with Magician action, often combined with overdose of ego – many variations on the general theme of 'God made in the image of man', such as the assumption that place is solely an extension of self*]

To bridge across to the Artist, focus on:

- what subtle changes do I notice from moment to moment in my feeling of connectedness with place?

To bridge across to the Scientist, focus on:

- in what ways is this same truth is shared by others?

To bridge across to the Magician (hardest), focus on:

- what practical use has this belief?
- is this belief appropriate for the purpose?

The discipline of the Mystic mode is probably the easiest to understand *as* discipline – a subtle, firm, delicate, precise, unwavering focus on *one* task at a time. It's probable that we choose that 'one true thing' in the Artist mode, we test it in the Scientist, and we apply it in the Magician; but we *live* it, express it with our whole being, in and as the Mystic.

This is the core of dowsing as a skill – in fact is common to *every* skill. Watch any experienced practitioner at work on any skill – from dowsing to glassblowing to tennis to trumpet-playing, or anything in between – and there, in the midst of all the activity, you'll see the exact same facial expression, the same quiet yet determined concentration. It's not 'control' as such – in fact any attempts at rigid control just get in the way. Instead, it's more about *focus*: a delicate dance, an intent intention on the task at hand, yet still aware of and open to any change, any possibility.

This condition of 'thinking narrow, being wide' is technically a state of light trance. The term 'trance' may worry some, so we'd perhaps better hasten to add that it's a *self*-induced light-trance, always as a conscious choice, and one which it's possible to leave at any moment. Indeed, that's actually the problem: it's all too easy to allow interruptions to cause us to bounce out of that state – and the quality of the work always suffers as a result. Hence the need for the discipline of the Mystic mode, to maintain that focus throughout the work-session, despite any distractions, disruptions and disturbances that might happen by.

One of the difficulties in talking about the Mystic mode is its unfortunate and often unwarranted association with religion: the latter somehow seems more to get in the way of spiritual experience rather than assist it...

So whilst, yes, we'd agree that the religious traditions do have their own role to play, there's still a real need for practical alternatives. One of our 'unsung heroes' in this is Colin Clark, whose work, in our view, sets the standard for developing Mystic-mode skills in a 'clean' context uncluttered by religious connotations. Drawing on key sources of research on behavioural modelling, such as *The Structure of Magic Vols. I & II* by Grinder and Bandler (the co-creators of NLP, or Neuro-Linguistic Programming), Clark provides simple step-by-step methods to develop, test and verify sensory awareness for so-called 'psychic skills' such as dowsing and direct-sensing. In effect, he uses the mode of the Magician to enhance the Mystic: kind of a contradiction in terms, in some ways, but it works – and works well.

Watch out for Clark's book and CD when it's published soon; in the meantime there's more detail on his website www.drawninward.com. Recommended, anyway.

We should perhaps note that that discipline of focus is about the closest we come in the Mystic mode to *doing* anything. Most of 'doing' is in the outer-value of the Magician mode, which is the diametric opposite; here in the Mystic it's all about inner-truth and inner meaning, and about 'revelations' that change that meaning. Hence, for the Mystic, the core principle that "the deeper truth will reveal itself".

The focus on 'higher Truth' also provides an important corollary to Gooch's Paradox, in the sometimes bizarre-seeming tactic that "to remember something you never knew, first set out to forget it". To do this in scientific research, for example, we would study the subject-area intently – literature-research, experimental data, anything and everything else we could lay our hands on in the Scientist mode – and then deliberately drop the whole thing for a while, with the casual-seeming wandering-off of the Artist. This tactic seems to create a kind of 'hologram' of the conceptual space populated by all the previous work in the Scientist mode. In 'forgetting', we then *trust* – trust being another characteristic of the Mystic mode – that at some point there will be some kind of trigger that causes the blurriness of the hologram to coalesce into a single brief yet sometimes almost blinding insight. Though often combined in some ways with the intentional not-so-randomness of the Artist, it's the Mystic's quietly-disciplined focus on 'higher Truth' – whatever that chosen 'higher Truth' may be – that creates the space for that insight to enter into awareness. Hence, again, the importance of this discipline in dowsing, which by its nature is so dependent on 'insights' of one kind or another.

Another key concern for dowsers is that the Mystic is the guardian of belief, which in turn is at the core of many – perhaps most – of the processes that trigger the dowsing response. In effect, we state, as a Magician, that it is 'true' that the instrument will respond in a particular way in specific context; we then hand it over to the Mystic to assert and ensure that that truth – and *only* that truth – will be the cause of the required response.

Hence "I believe that the rods will cross over above a water-line, and *only* cross above such a line", and so on; and hence, too, the problems that can arise when that belief is blown out of the water by an aggressive Skeptic – or equally by an overly 'helpful' colleague who insists, "That's wrong – you have to do it *this* way!"

> And hence also an amusing clash which was reported some years back at a conference of the British Society of Dowsers. The speaker was a water-engineer who'd been supervising repairs to water-mains up in the north of England. They routinely used dowsing to find problem-areas in the pipes – in their experience it was more reliable than the rather limited electronic sensors of the time. As far as they knew, dowsing could only be used to find water.
>
> But on one job, out on the docks, they met up with the dockside electricians – who also used dowsing, and who were equally convinced that it could only be used to find buried cables. Instant panic on either side: "you mean we could have hit a water main?" "be far worse if *we* hit a live cable!" But in fact it had never happened before, because of their belief in the exclusivity of the skill – though for a while they actually *were* at risk, while their beliefs were so shaken up by the incident…
>
> Belief *matters* here: guard it carefully with the Mystic mode.

The Mystic maintains the separation between 'true' and 'not-true', 'in' versus 'out', and for that matter between 'sacred' and 'pro-fane'. In reality it's somewhat arbitrary, but it doesn't *feel* that way – in fact shouldn't, if the Mystic is to do its work well. Within that mode, the Mystic maintains our *connection* with truth. It's also key in our connection with place – the sense of 'connectedness', of *belonging* in and to and with a place.

This connectedness is actually the root of that Welsh word *cynefin* – and the Cynefin model we mentioned earlier (see p.20) makes even more sense if you think of that way. Western culture's focus on analysis, on slicing everything apart into ever smaller partitions, tends to create a sense of alienation, of disconnection from people and from place. But as Colin Clark puts it, the disconnect is not real: it's an artefact of analysis – of the Scientist, not the Mystic. It's essential not to confuse the two disciplines here: in the Mystic mode, only the connection is real.

> There's a domain called 'spiritual dowsing' that should in principle be of value here, because it purports to enhance that sense of connection between people and place. But at present, sadly, its methods are so often presented in such an undisciplined manner – a random mishmash of Artist and Mystic, without any balance from the Scientist or Magician – that in practice it's often more of a hindrance than a help.
>
> At times it can be a lot *worse* than just a hindrance. As we've mentioned elsewhere, we've seen way too many appalling incidents of so-called 'spirituality' in dowsing – and some of those misuses have been downright dangerous, especially in supposed 'earth-healing' and management of geopathic stress. So for safety reasons, if nothing else – see the Reality Risk (p.82) – we would urge you to apply any such ideas only with extreme caution.
>
> A pity, though, because spiritual discipline *is* sorely needed in dowsing. Oh well…

The Mystic mode is more at risk of such problems, too, because it connects with some very real and very human yearnings. The glamour of the New Age *is* sometimes relevant and useful here, because it's so often the starting-point with which people first connect. That initial hunger for the surface-level glamour should, with luck, move on to a hunger for something more real, a deeper, more *personal* quest for meaning. Between the two, there may well be a painful stage of bitter disenchantment, a bleak question of "is this really *all* there is?"; yet that too should – again, with luck – soon move on something more like "what is it that *means* something, that rings true for me?".

Yet here, as every mystical tradition would warn us, we meet up with the greatest 'enemy' of the Mystic mode: ego. In short, all our hopes, our desires, our fears, our need to be noticed, and so on, and on, and on… every aspect of ourselves where we place 'I' at –

and as – the centre of attention. And unfortunately the hype and glamour and Golden-Age myths of the less honest end of the New Age feed right into that problem of ego. Worse, its glamour is addictive, because it promises so much, but can never actually deliver: all it *can* deliver is an ersatz 'deeper truth', a kind of flaccid 'truth-without-tears' rather than the painful truths on the far side of the 'Dark Night of the Soul'. The problem is that only the latter is real, but we so, so much want the glamour to be real instead…

Sorry, folks, but whether we like it or not, the only way out of this one is the hard work of a real discipline, together with a hefty dose of humility. And the discipline of the Mystic in dowsing is threefold: maintain the focus on the instrument – whatever that might be; maintain the beliefs that are used to trigger responses from the instrument; and maintain that sense of connectedness with place. Anything else supposedly 'spiritual' may well be a distraction here: and that's a useful fact to bear in mind as we work.

THE DOWSER AS SCIENTIST

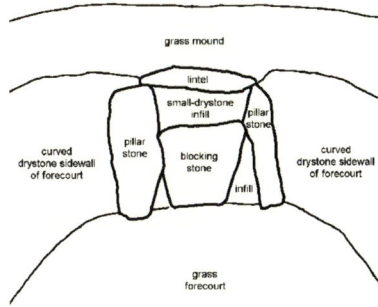

The diagram labels: grass mound, lintel, small-drystone infill, pillar stone, pillar stone, curved drystone sidewall of forecourt, pillar stone, blocking stone, infill, curved drystone sidewall of forecourt, grass forecourt

Principles...

Unlike many other intuitive skills, a key characteristic of dowsing is about linking its sensing to an *identified location*. The location may be physical – literally out in a field somewhere – or virtual – on a map, a diagram, a chart or some other kind of representation. The closer to physical, the easier and more reliable the work is likely to be, but the type doesn't actually matter - in principle at least. What *does* matter is that there's some clear, explicit means to identify that location at each moment during the work.

So like a scientist, there's a key emphasis here on *fact* – particularly as it relates to location. There's also an emphasis on *definition*, to identify shared meaning of terms and values – though again, this will be more consistent when the work is in a physical context.

Like the Mystic, the focus here is on 'truth'; yet unlike the Mystic, that 'truth' is not arbitrarily declared, but must be anchored in analysis, cross-linking everything to everything else to create a firm foundation for fact. So the appropriate Cynefin tactic here is 'sense / analyse / respond': slow, cautious, careful, measured in every sense of the word, because a single missed step could bring down the whole structure into ridicule and ruin. In that sense, amongst all of the various 'sins' of dubious discipline, the Scientist mode is most at risk of the Meaning Mistake (see p.65).

A scientist might say "I serve the truth", yet it's a quiet, almost dispassionate truth, with none of the emotional loading that we see in the capitalised '*the* Truth' of the Mystic mode. In that sense, it aims to be objective rather than subjective. The key mechanism for this is the *peer review*: other people must be able to identify the same facts and repeat the same results under the same conditions.

That, however, is the catch: 'the same conditions'. Often in dowsing we don't *know* what all of the applicable conditions may be in a given context - especially where the 'equation of need' may be involved – so it can be difficult to work out what can be repeated, and what can't. And unless it *can* be repeated, it isn't science.

Still, we do what we can. The Scientist mode works best when it restricts itself to physical fact – a key point in archaeology dowsing, where deriving dates by dowsing is a known problem. What's needed instead are measurements and coordinates that *can* be anchored to some specific, identified frame: a map-grid, a house-plan, a baseline or reference-standard, or, on the body, some physical identifier such as a vertebra-number or name of muscle. In *this* mode, anything unanchored in that sense is likely to be a waste of energy and time.

Despite the focus on fact, scientists do have their own artistic expression, even their own form of beauty. It tends, though, to be emphasised in abstraction, the clean elegance of an equation, a map, a technical diagram or an isometric projection – anything which makes it possible to share meaning in an objective manner.

The dowser as scientist… measuring, mapping, *finding facts* in the physical world.

…and practice

The role of the Scientist mode is to *verify* the truth of things in relation to others.

The Scientist manages that which is inherently *knowable* – a world in which everything is interlinked through complicated connections of cause and effect.

The Scientist responds to the context through a sense of *outer truth*, measuring, monitoring, and assessing the factors that make up the chains of interrelationship, with a decision-sequence of sense → analyse → respond.

You'll need to use the Scientist discipline when:

- you need to identify the location, and changes in location
- you need to verify what is fact, and what is not
- you need to compare results from previous sessions, or record results to cross-reference in other sessions
- you need to describe results in ways that can be interpreted in a factual senses by others, and cross-referenced to those of others

- you are creating some kind of theoretical scheme to describe what you've discovered

You'll know you're in the Scientist mode when:

- there's a focus on location – *where* something is happening
- there's a focus on measurement and 'fact'
- you're analysing what's happening or has happened

Rules that apply in the Scientist discipline include:

- only facts are real – opinion is permitted only where vetted and verified by peer-review
- everything must be anchored to everything else
- everything must ultimately be anchored in shared standards
- proof depends on repeatability – especially repeatability by others
- things are true only if verified in formal logic
- experiments should change only one parameter at a time
- all variable parameters must be identified and declared

Warning-signs of dubious Scientist discipline include:

- emotional attachment to any supposed 'fact' *[blurring Scientist with one or more other modes, usually the Mystic]*
- "must be…", "obviously…", "of course…" *[failure to bridge across to Artist or Magician for cross-checks against 'logic-holes']*
- "the exception proves the rule…" *[blurring Scientist (strict logic) with Magician (practicality, 'rules of thumb')]*
- "the only possible truth…" *[blurring Scientist (analysis) with Mystic (only one Truth, without question)]*

To bridge across to the Mystic, focus on:

- what is *true* in an objective sense? what would change a theory to 'scientific law'?
- what is constant here? what are the incontrovertible standards?
- what absolute boundaries exist between 'true' and 'not-true' – how do I remove doubts about any possible 'shades of grey'?

To bridge across to the Magician, focus on:

- what is 'applied science'? – what is the practical *use* of these theories or analyses?

- how may I check against dubious discipline? – particularly against going 'half-baked' or 'overcooked' in the Meaning Mistake?

To bridge across to the Artist (hardest), focus on:

- what ideas and experiences would provide me with the new data I need?
- how can I break out of 'stuckness'?

The Scientist mode provides us with two disciplines of 'objective truth' that we need in dowsing: precision of measurement, and precision of thought. The catch is that we need the first *during* a work-session, though not that much thereafter; and we need the latter both *before* and *after* a session, but also need to be careful not to let it intrude inappropriately during the session itself. This can call for some interesting mental juggling on the dowser's part...

Throughout the Scientist mode, the emphasis is on establishing known fact. Within the actual practice of dowsing, the key fact that we need is that of location: put simply, we need to know at all times the answer to the question "where am I?" – and know the precision of that answer, too. So we'll usually need some kind of coordinate system, or map-reference, or other means to identify precisely where we are in the respective space – and keep track of those coordinates as we move around. In field-dowsing, the location would usually be physical – we could track it with a GPS, perhaps, or survey-poles, or whatever – but in principle there's no reason to restrict ourselves solely to that: many dowsers are happy to work from maps, for example, and do it well. The point here is that there needs to be some definite, explicit and unambiguous means to identify and track the location of each dowsing response. In other words, we need to ensure that that location is *fact*: hence the need for the Scientist.

Locations in space are relatively straightforward: there are well-established survey-techniques that will handle that all of that (see p.101), and as long as we take care to follow the respective rules, we'll end up with the requisite facts. Some techniques are more precise than others: a GPS track is quick and easy, but to get the accuracy needed for a drilling-rig or an archaeology dig – the kind of precision that water-diviners and archaeological dowsers will routinely achieve – you'll need a proper triangulated survey using tapes and levels. There are plenty of practical complications, par-ticularly in mapping paths and directions of water-flows and the like, but that's mostly a matter of detail – something at which the Scientist mode excels.

What's *not* so simple is dowsing for dates, or anything else that's virtual or abstract. The point here – which far too many dowsers seem to miss, even though it's hardly a subtle one – is that as soon as we move outside of the usual three dimensions, we're no longer in the realm of fact: we're in the realms of guesswork or belief – blurring into the mode of Magician or Mystic respectively. We need to *know* if and when we've done so, and act accordingly, as explored later in the section on integration (see p.61); but if instead we pretend we're still solely in the realm of the Scientist, we'll end up with results that are meaningless at best. Which, once again. kind of defeats the object of the exercise...

> One of the quickest ways we know to annoy an archaeologist is to dowse for dates, and then insist that those imagined dates are fact. Don't do it!
>
> It's slightly more reliable if you can use a physical object as a 'sample' to represent a date – a flint arrowhead as a sample for Neolithic-period artefacts in general, for example – but even then it's still somewhat dubious and easily disputed. The simplest guideline is that if you can't *prove* something is fact in a strict scientific sense, don't claim that it is.

The same applies to what we look for, and the methods we use to define what we're looking for: the further we go from the phys-ical, the less reliable it gets. Once again, this is hardly a subtle point, yet it's disturbing how many dowsers seem to fail to realise that there's a *lot* of difference between dowsing for a broken drain with a sample of drain-pipe in hand, versus searching for some unspecified 'earth-energy' by a supposed 'signature', counting out the number of turns clockwise and counter-clockwise on a pen-dulum, or simply by holding the word in mind whilst working. The drain-pipe is concrete fact – perhaps literally so – whilst the 'energy' is not; likewise the means used to search for each. There's a continuum here, of course, but the cut-off point for the Scientist mode on its own occurs as soon as we move away from physical fact. Beyond that point, we'll necessarily find ourselves juggling between two or more modes at the same time – which is where it *definitely* gets tricky...

In short, if you can't hear it, see it, scent it, taste it, touch it – or use a physical instrument to do so for you by proxy, as scientists do – then it ain't fact. Nothing wrong in that, because imaginary energies and the like *are* entirely real, in their own peculiar ways.

But they're not 'real' in any way that the Scientist can handle on its own: they're either an experience – for which we'd call in the Artist – or an opinion – for which enter the Magician, the Mystic, or both.

The classic example of a bridge between the Artist and Scientist is Robert Pirsig's 'fishing for facts' (see p.33). This is a discipline in itself, as Pirsig describes in his book; Beveridge describes many others in *The Art of Scientific Investigation*; and both would seem to be near-essential reference-books for dowsers here.

By contrast, when working with the Scientist, the Mystic and Magician simply *declare* that some opinions are better than others. (The Mystic calls this 'peer-review', whilst the Magician calls it 'best practice', with somewhat more reason for doing so, but it comes to much the same in the end.) The key outcome for such declarations is a set of agreed reference-standards, which include such things as taxonomies and naming-standards – essential items for cross-reference that are at last beginning to make an appearance in the dowsing field, in the form of standards such as the British Society of Dowsers Earth Energy Group's *Encyclopaedia of Terms*. The one key point to remember here is that although agreement on a name for something does make it easier for different people to describe and cross-reference their experiences of that thing, it still doesn't tell us what that thing *is*: it's just a name, not the thing itself. The map is not the territory.

But names and standards are essential for the other discipline of the Scientist mode: precision of thought. Whilst the Mystic will declare something to be true, as a matter of faith and belief, the Scientist needs to arrive at its 'truth' by a formal process of reasoning and logic.

> It's perhaps worth pointing out some subtle limitations to Scientist logic that those of a New Age mindset may not know, whilst those of a Skeptic persuasion often prefer to ignore.
>
> It's impressive what can be done with a fully anchored logic-chain – create understandings of almost anything from the moment of the Big Bang to the chemistry of neuron-switching in the brain – but the hard fact remains that every one of these chains is ultimately grounded in assumptions. We know there are (at least) four distinct forces in the universe – weak nuclear, strong nuclear, gravitational, electromagnetic – but in honesty we have no idea what any of them actually *are*. It's a mystery: one that neither logic nor science can explain. For now, anyway.

Logic is also extremely fragile. It's always dependent on the validity of its assumptions – for which it has no means within itself to test. And as we'll see later, it's always at risk of the Meaning Mistake – a single missed factor, or a single missed step in the logic, can invalidate the entire edifice. Not a fact that's easy to live with – hence, perhaps, why Skeptics are so keen to point out the mistakes of others, because doing so can distract attention from their own…

And whilst logic is excellent for explaining how or what or when or where, it's all but useless for explaining *why*. We know what many constants are, for example, yet often no have idea why they have that specific value, or even why they *are* constant. In many sciences, and to many scientists, the study of 'why' – teleology – is almost a dirty word: a taboo subject, because they have no way to handle it. Which does *not*, however, mean it doesn't exist…

Then there's that limitation in the link between physics and fact. The Scientist could tell us (in probabilistic terms, at least) how many atoms dance on the head of a pin, but not how many angels or other nominally-imaginary entities and energies – and as dowsers, it may well be the latter that we need to know about.

In short, the Scientist mode is useful – but it's not the be-all-and-end-all sole-guardian-of-truth that Skeptics and some scientists like to pretend it is. Use it with care.

Formal logic is unforgiving: a strict *"if* this, *therefore* that"*. There's no tolerance for error: every step must be anchored to some other known fact, every inch of the way. To the Scientist, 'logic-holes' are as much anathema as doubt and difference are to the Mystic.

The other unforgiving requirement is repeatability: for a fact to become 'objective', it must be possible for others to repeat the same test and arrive at the same result. Which is where standards and common nomenclature come in: without them, there's no way to identify whether two things that are supposedly the same really *are* the same. This is as true for dowsers as for everyone else: if we want our results to be meaningful to anyone else – to move out from the personal 'subjective' layer of the Artist and the Mystic, and up into the shared space of the Scientist and the Magician – we need common meanings, structured records and the rest.

Which is, again, where the Scientist mode comes to our aid. We need to plan for repeatability *before* a work-session: we need to know what it is that we're looking for, we need to know where it is that we'll be looking, and how to identify each location. And we'll need the same *after* a session, to verify what it is that we've found, and where we found it.

> Where we *don't* want any of this is *during* a session: the 'I got it here last time so it ought to be here this time' mistake is perhaps the most common dowsing error there is....

We need structure for all of this; we need consistency, both in the planning and the execution, if we're going to be able to derive any meaning from the results we obtain in our dowsing work. There's a lot we can learn from the Scientist – and need to learn, too.

Yet there is one more catch with the Scientist mode of which we need to beware. As a friend of ours put it, "scientists are like people in wheelchairs: they need firm level ground to move about on". In the process of levelling, though, *everything* is levelled out, levelled up to a highest common factor, levelled down to a lowest common denominator, and so on. The ground itself is changed: the map matches the territory only because the territory itself has been reduced to an abstraction that matches the map. Just how 'real' or 'true' this may be in any ultimate sense is an interesting question...

In search of certainty, the Scientist aims to level out all possible uncertainties. Yet as science itself shows us, the world *is* uncertain, and inherently so; there *are* many things that don't repeat; chaos is real. There's no way that the Scientist mode can make sense of that: it's outside of its milieu, outside of its scope. So to make sense of chaos – to make *use* of that chaos – we need turn to the last mode: the Magician.

THE DOWSER
AS MAGICIAN

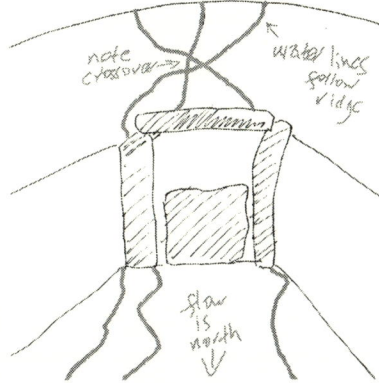

Principles...

The end-point of all dowsing
work is something that is of *use*.
The purpose may be something
like practical – finding a blockage in a drain, perhaps, or in an
artery – or it may be more personal, a quest for knowledge or
revelation: but there's still always some purpose in mind.

Like a technologist, or a magician, our aim here is to *do* something
– "the art and science of causing change conformity with will", as
one perhaps infamous writer once put it.

As that phrase suggests, this mode is something of a bridge
between the Artist and the Scientist. Like the latter, the work is
grounded in studied action, often though by no means always in
the physical world; but like the former, we accept that the world
we work in is inherently uncertain. So the appropriate Cynefin
tactic here is 'probe / sense / respond': we try some small
experiment, see what we get, and try again, working closer and
closer to the desired result.

There *is* a kind of 'truth' here, but it's more in the form of "I serve
the truth of the purpose". The real focus here is more on value, on
usefulness, on results that have practical worth in the outer world.
This in turn depends on a constant emphasis on improvements in
effectiveness: is it efficient? is it reliable? is it elegant? appropriate?
integrated with everything else?

In practice most new techniques start off as a mad idea or experience
of the Artist; we then need the Magician to ensure that it doesn't get
stuck in the over-certainty of the Mystic, as "*the* way to do it".

For example, in the early part of the last century, dowsing reports
would often include phrases such as "using a green pendulum – for it
was raining", implying that the colour was a critical factor. It's taken a
few decades of the Magician's experiments to learn that in most cases
the colour doesn't matter at all: more a matter of aesthetics or
personal preference than of operational essentials.

It's the same in everyday technologies, though. For centuries it was thought that hardening of steel for mill-bills and other stone-cutting tools was dependent on the mixture into which the hot metal was quenched. Only after decades of careful experiment – in the real everyday work of the Magician, not in the Scientist's laboratory – was it finally understood that almost any low-viscosity liquid will work as the quenching-mixture: the one really critical factor is the temperature of the steel when it's quenched.

The Magician depends on constant questioning, constant reflective doubt – the exact opposite of the Mystic's certainty. Get the job done, achieve the required results, yet always ask whether it could be done differently, more effectively, done a better way: that's the role of the Magician.

The problem with the Magician, perhaps, is that it can be difficult for others to follow what's happening. Since it's highly dependent on personal skill – and hence always at risk of getting lost in the skills-learning labyrinth (see p.87) – a surprising amount of what's done will be as personal as the Artist. And whilst the Scientist can only cope with changes in one parameter at a time, the Magician needs to achieve its required results, regardless of what's going on, in conditions which are often one-off or unrepeatable, at least in part. In short, it's sometimes hard to work out what's going on, and often even harder to explain. To paraphrase Arthur C Clarke, any sufficiently advanced magic is indistinguishable from technology – but it still looks like magic to the rest of us...

The focus for the Magician is always on application, effectiveness, use – and that applies to its aesthetics, too. Like the Scientist, there's usually a high degree of abstraction; but the aim is usually more *illustrative*, to explain some point of practice.

The dowser as technologist, as magician... applying ideas in practice for a useful purpose in the everyday world.

...and practice

The role of the Magician mode is to *use*, and to *question* use and usefulness.

The Magician manages that which is inherently *complex* – always somewhat uncertain, requiring endless adaptation, and with cause and effect often identifiable only in retrospect.

The Magician responds to the context through a sense of *outer value*, experimenting to find whatever feels appropriate for its needs, with a decision-sequence of probe → sense → respond.

You'll need to use the Magician discipline when:

- you apply outcomes from other modes to practical use
- you need to adapt practice to the specific context
- you need to review value, or to question what you're doing in practice – particularly around quality and effectiveness, overall or in a given context
- you need to assess any kind of trade-off or risk – from ethics or health and safety to the practicalities of dowsing in a public place or negotiating with farmers for access to a field

You'll know you're in the Magician mode when:

- the focus is on practical, useful results
- the focus is on any kind of trade-off or risk-assessment
- you're dealing with patterns or clusters of some kind of one-off or special-case

Rules that apply in the Magician discipline include:

- there is no 'truth' – only usefulness, or not-usefulness
- beliefs, feelings, objects, facts, everything is a tool to a purpose
- 'as above, so below' – everything contains everything else, reality is fractal, self-similar, recursive – hence analogy and metaphor are as likely to be useful as logic or 'proof'
- the LEARN acronym for effectiveness: is it elegant, efficient, appropriate, reliable, integrated?
- ethics and integrity take priority over 'truth' – I am personally responsible for the consequences of what I do and not-do

Warning-signs of dubious Magician discipline include:

- "*the* way to do it is…" *[blurring Magician with Mystic or Scientist]*
- "it'll be the same as last time…" *[blurring Magician with Scientist]*
- "the end justifies the means…" *[allowing Mystic 'truth' to override value-assessment]*
- "get the job out of the door any way we can – they won't notice the difference…" *[weak handling of values trade-offs, also failure to bridge across to Scientist and Artist to assist in improving quality]*

- "I'm no good at...", "I'm the best at..." *[allowing ego to override the Magician's responsibility to test and question everything]*

To bridge across to the Scientist, focus on:

- how should I analyse these results?
- how do these results compare with previous times or similar contexts, or with results from others?
- what kind of measurements or formal standards should I use?

To bridge across to the Artist, focus on:

- what new ideas or new information do I need?
- how can we make this more interesting, more engaging, more fun?

To bridge across to the Mystic (hardest), focus on:

- what inner discipline do I need here?
- in using beliefs as tools, how do I hold fast to a belief?
- what is the 'Higher Truth' here? – what ethics and morals apply here? what is 'the Law' in this context?

Of all the modes, only the Magician has any real interest in *doing*, in concrete action, in creating useful change. The Artist provides the ideas and experiences; the Mystic provides the connection and focus; the Scientist provides the framework in which things can make sense; but it's the Magician who finally puts it all to practical use.

Two key themes to explore here are *best-practice* and *worst-practice*. Between them they describe a continuum of the ways in which we can learn from others, and learn from our own 'mis-takes', to improve our competencies and skills. This continuum is a kind of bridge between Scientist and Artist, with Magician in the middle: though note that the emphasis here is always on *practice* – not theory, as it would be for the Scientist, or experience for its own sake, as it would be for the Artist.

Best-practice sits more toward the Scientist end of that bridge. The accent here is on repeatability – what other people have found works best in the same conditions. So the key concern in this case is in identifying what the conditions are, and hence whether that previous best-practice would apply in *this* context, here, now. If the conditions are only similar, what would need to be changed to gain the same best value? From a dowser's perspective, this applies most at the physical end of the spectrum of practice – pipes and drains, rather than imaginary entities or earth-energies

– and more in the early stages of skills-development, too, before the skill necessarily develops into something more personal and unique.

Worst-practice sits more toward the Artist end of the bridge. The accent here is on uniqueness, on what is *not* repeatable, and the processes we and others go through to cope with that difference and uncertainty. The usual first try is best-practice, following our training; but when that doesn't work, then what do we do? This is where Pirsig's comments about 'gumption' start to make real *practical* sense. The Artist can help a lot here, too: every 'side-feeling' in a dowsing-session is a clue that there's something else to know, perhaps some other way to do it better. But perhaps the first liberation here is a realisation that it isn't just us - everyone else gets it 'wrong' too, everyone has difficulties making it work according to 'the official method'. And whilst the more skilled practitioners make it all look so easy, fact is that they're in the same boat too, struggling with uncertainty and the rest – worse so than us, in many ways, because they're so much further out over the edge than we are in terms of the challenges they face.

Best-practice is about defining what works; worst-practice is about sharing stories of what doesn't, and building communities of practice in which it's safe to admit that it *is* hard, that we *do* get it wrong sometimes – often? – and in which we work together to find new ways to make it work, in ever-changing, ever more complex conditions. Interesting…

> Also interesting in this light is a relatively recent branch of study called 'chaos magic'. Like the Artist, the core principle is 'anything goes' – but in chaos-magic this principle becomes a matter of deliberate *practice*, rather than the Artist's rather more random experience.
>
> The idea is this: that we choose a belief, and act as if it is absolutely true in every possible way – yet keep a tiny portion of the mind to one side that knows that this a choice, that could be changed at a moment's notice, any time we choose. So we hold each belief with the intensity of the Mystic, but switch beliefs with the speed of the Artist, in accordance with the Magician's emphasis on purpose and usefulness. In effect, a technology of belief; belief *as* technology.
>
> It's actually the same principle as used in affirmations and the like: we affirm that something is 'true' - even though we know it's not true, at the time – yet by acting accordingly, it *becomes* true. The difference here – or extension, rather – is that in chaos magic it's applied not just to a few beliefs, but to *everything*; and it's done as a fully-fledged technology – complete with its own best-practice and worst-practice –

> rather than the typically rather woolly, blurry, indefinite descriptions that come out the usual New Age context.
>
> Probably the best reference on this is the anonymous book *SSOTBME*, though Tom's book *Inventing Reality* extends the same principles in a form that may be easier for many readers. At the very least, recommended as an eye-opener for dowsers, introducing a very different yet very usable way to re-think their own craft.

Whilst the Scientist is concerned with 'truth', and asks "How does it work?" – to which the ultimate answer, *always*, is "dunno…" – the emphasis for the technologist or Magician is "How can it be worked?" – which is not the same question at all. Throughout this mode, the driving question is "What works?", or perhaps even more, "How can it work *better*?" Those are the questions that the disciplines of best-practice and worst-practice aim to answer.

The acronym 'LEARN' can be useful here, in tackling "how can it work better?". It provides a checklist of the dimensions that we need to watch as we work in the Magician mode:

- e*L*egant – how well does this support the human factors in the skill, the subtle differences in personal needs and personal responses?
- *E*fficient – how well does this make the best use of the available energies and resources?
- *A*ppropriate – how well does this method or approach support the overall purpose? – the procedure, policy, principles, and overall vision for the work?
- *R*eliable – how well can this method or approach be relied upon to deliver the required results?
- i*N*tegrated- how well does this method or approach help to link those other dimensions together into a unified whole?

In each case, those questions help to challenge us to improve the *usefulness* of dowsing practice. Whatever we do, we could *always* do it better: that's one of the ways the Magician mode will help.

> We also need the Magician to tackle the 'So what?' question – what's the point, what's the use, what's in it for me? It's only here, really, that we have a real answer to the timewasting tactics of people like the Skeptics: before they've finished pontificating about what is 'true according to Science' and the rest, we should have already found the blocked drain, dug a hole, sorted out the mess, cleaned up and gone home. When you can do that for real, reliably, day after day, dowsing starts to *matter* to everyday folk… In other words, you have a definite answer to "So what?"

One of the annoyances for mathematicians is what's called 'numerics': items that are obviously a matter of excitement for whoever discovers them, but in reality are little more than glorified coincidences, and of little or no practical use. You've discovered that every multiple of nine also adds up to nine, you say? Fascinating – but so what?

And there are all too many equivalent annoyances in dowsing and earth-mysteries. For example, almost any of us could stare at maps for a while, seeing all manner of interesting coincidences. We might then search intently for other items that seem to match that pattern – even though that's exactly what *not* to do in the Scientist mode. And if we fail to follow it up with fieldwork, there's no way to verify it in the real world, so it can never move past that level of 'interesting coincidence'. Nothing for the Artist; nothing for the Magician either; could perhaps be of interest to a misguided Mystic, but otherwise no *use* whatsoever. You've discovered an example of that perfect contradiction-in-terms, the circular alignment, you say? Fascinating – but so what?

"So what?" If you want your work to be credible to others, be ready to answer that question; and make sure – with the Magician's help – that you have a good answer, too.

A final point here, perhaps, is about the primacy of ethics. There's probably no such thing as 'black magic', or 'white magic' for that matter, but there's certainly an endless spectrum of shades of grey – and ethics is the deciding factor as to which end of that spectrum we face. The world of the Magician is one of outer-value, not inner-truth; this is ethics not just talked about, or theorised about, or prayed about, but *lived* as a matter of practice, in every decision, however, trivial, however small. As we saw back in *A question of quality*, on p.20, the root of all quality-management is vision; and vision is ultimately anchored in ethics.

The Mystic may well see the Magician as amoral at best; but to the Magician, the Mystic's morals are just a package of predefined answers, little more than a lazy-man's ethics for an imaginary, idealised world which, unrealistically, is assumed to be certain, known, proven, 'true'. In the inherently *un*certain world that the Magician inhabits, where the 'equation of need' is often a critical factor in the process, ethics is *hard*; and *every* decision is an ethical one.

So ethics *matters* to dowsers – perhaps far more than most seem to realise, from our observation of the field over the past few decades. As we move now to explore how to weave all the modes together into a single unified whole, it might well be worth while keeping that point in mind.

THE INTEGRATED DOWSER

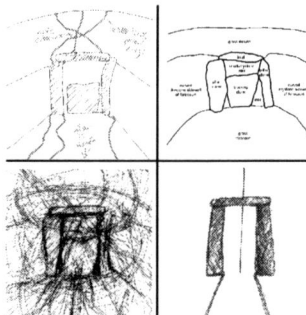

Principles...

Each of the modes has its own role –
the Artist, Mystic, Scientist and Magician. Yet none of them can do all of what we need in dowsing, and much of the time they're mutually exclusive. The real skill, then, is to weave each of these disciplines together in real time in a way that works as a unified whole.

Each discipline has its own rules: yet since they're often mutually exclusive, only one set of rules can apply at any one time. So the aim is to switch between the modes, moment by moment, and *know* which discipline and rules are being used at that moment. Unless we get this right, we'll inevitably find ourselves in one or other of the 'sins' – and quality will suffer as a result. Integration *matters*.

In terms of quality-management, the disciplines provide the 'procedures' layer, defining and redefining the 'work-instructions' in use moment by moment. As a guide:

- emphasise the Artist to focus on the processes of *sensing* – what am I feeling in this moment? what are the rods doing right now? how must I express this?
- emphasise the Mystic to keep track of *belief*, and to build a sense of *belonging* – what am I looking for right now? what will the rods do when I find it? how am I connecting with this place?
- emphasise the Scientist to note *location*, and to verify *fact* – where exactly is this place? in reference to what coordinates, what baseline? how should I record this?
- emphasise the Magician to link *action* to *purpose* – am I on track? am I on time? am I doing what needs to be done? is this efficient, reliable, elegant, appropriate? could I do this a better way?

For the given dowsing task, you'll also need to assign just one of the modes as the 'policy' layer, to provide a reference-point in case of any 'dispute' between the modes. For example, if you're aiming to find a water-supply or a blocked drain, you would emphasise the technologist, the Magician – and not allow yourself to wander off into the feelings of the Artist, or get hung up on the beliefs of the Mystic. To map out the defensive ditch and berm of an Iron Age site, you would probably emphasise the Scientist over the Magician, because location would be the key concern there. At other times – a first exploration of a site, perhaps – you might give priority to the Artist; and if a quest for 'revelation' matters most, or a sense of connection with place, you might focus more on the Mystic. None of the disciplines is necessarily 'better' than any of the others: it all depends on what you aim to do.

Above all of these, though, there's the 'vision' layer – the overall 'guiding star' for quality-management. Much of this will be personal – it's your *own* guiding-star, not necessarily anyone else's. Yet it should, and must, always include a code of personal and professional ethics – respect for people and for place, in the broadest sense of each – and also remain aware of health and safety and the like, again in the broadest sense.

The integrated dowser... weaving disciplines and layers together into a unified whole.

...and practice

So how *do* we weave the disciplines together in the day-to-day practice of dowsing?

Well, that's a discipline in itself, for which the simplest description would be to point back to the lists in the 'Practice' section for each discipline (see p.30 for Artist, p.39 for Mystic, p.46 for Scientist, and p.54 for Magician). Each list is structured as follows:

- the overall role of the discipline
- the type of 'world' which the discipline would address
- the core emphasis and response for the discipline
- when to use the discipline
- how to identify when you're already using that discipline
- rules that apply within the discipline
- warning-signs of problems with that discipline
- ways to bridge across to the other disciplines

We can then use the lists in a variety of different ways, forwards, backwards, crosslinking between them, and so on. For example:

Which mode am I in right now? – look at the roles, or the 'You'll know you're in...' lists, or work it out backwards from the rules that you're using at present.

If I'm in this mode, what rules apply? – look them up from the respective list – and check the 'warning signs' list to check if you're blurring them with the rules from another mode.

Which mode do I need to be in? – look at the 'You'll need to use when...' lists, and pick out the appropriate mode according to the task at hand – and remember to use that new mode's rules and tactics, not continue to use the rules for the current mode!

If I'm in this mode, how do I switch cleanly to another mode? – look at the 'bridge' lists for suggestions – though note that switching to the diametrically-opposite mode may well seem hard at first.

Let's see a quick example of how this works in practice.

You're out in the field, keeping the focus on the dowsing-rods with the discipline of the Mystic. The purpose of the work is held quietly in the background with the discipline of the Magician, to watch the overall 'doing' of the work – but in the moment-to-moment process of sensing with the rods, the Mystic is to the fore.

So the ongoing tactic here is sense → categorise → respond. You keep the focus, watching for any movement of the rods – the 'sense' part. You categorise each movement as 'relevant' or 'not relevant', according to the current search-pattern. And respond accordingly.

If it's categorised as 'relevant', you'd either put in a marker at that point, or quickly switch over to the Scientist to mark the location. The tactic in the Scientist mode is sense → analyse → respond: note the relationship to the fixed reference-baseline, calculate the coordinates, and record the result. As soon as that's finished, you switch straight back to the Mystic: stop analysing, and go back to the Mystic's focus, ready at an instant to sense and categorise again.

A 'side-feeling' comes through into your awareness. (See p.113 for typical examples, though there are an infinite variety of others, of course.) You don't try to categorise this side-feeling: instead, you switch smoothly into the Artist mode, where the appropriate tactic is act → sense → respond. Typically, in the middle of a dowsing session, the 'action' here is simply to *notice* the side-feeling; then use the senses to describe it in some way, and make an appropriate record as the response. But don't allow yourself to get distracted by the Artist. As soon as it's done, switch back to the task at hand, with the Mystic: sense, categorise, respond.

When that particular part of the work is complete, loosen off the focus of the Mystic, and switch to the Magician to assess what you've

---

done. How well did it work? Did you get the results you need, results you can use? Is there another way to do it better? Try another experiment, perhaps? So you'd use the Magician's tactic of probe → sense → respond at a slightly larger scale: probe the context with each experiment, each piece of practice; sense by assessing the results at each stage; and respond by setting up another piece of work, perhaps calling on the Scientist for advice on best-practice, or the Artist for worst-practice or for new ideas.

When you're all done for the day, call on the Scientist once more to make sure that everything is complete. − checklists for records and documentation, for ensuring that all the equipment is packed away with nothing left behind, and so on. Perhaps also ask the Scientist to analyse the results, compare with other sessions, or work done by others at different times or in different places.

Every mode is in use here; every mode has its role to play. Each very different in its approach, its tactics, yet switching between each in turn, as appropriate, within the work as an integrated whole.

None of this difficult, once we realise that the integration *drives* the choice of mode at each moment. All we have to do is keep track of which mode is needed, which mode is in use, and follow the respective rules that each mode requires.

And we can do it the other way round, too: we can choose a sequence of modes, and follow that path, changing the rules as we go. The classic example is the sequence that supposedly underpins all science: idea → hypothesis → theory → law. In our terms here, that's Artist, then Magician, then Scientist, and finally the Mystic: do something – anything, almost at random – to shake out a few ideas; probe with an experiment or two to test each hypothesis about those ideas; analyse the results of each hypothesis to create some kind of theory about how it works; and settle it into scientific law that can be used to categorise future events. An engineer, though, might well do things in the opposite order: chase up some new ideas; test them against different beliefs or laws ("is light made up of waves or particles? it all depends on what you want to do"); derive some kind of theory out of that; and put it to use as 'applied science'. Each to their own, really.

There's a useful analogy here with what's known in the IT industry as a 'mashup': link together disparate themes and technologies into a unified whole that can be used for something different, something new. Musicians work in a similar way with samples and re-mixes; and life as a whole does much the same, of course, constantly renewing itself through DNA's endless possibilities and permutations.

Re-combine, re-mix, re-purpose, re-use: that's the idea here.

So there are any number of ways we can do this: it all depends on what we're aiming to do. And the same switching of modes also applies at every level in the quality-system, from the moment-by-moment 'work-instruction', to its defining procedure, the guiding policy and the overall vision. It's all one continuum, one hologram, one integrated whole.

There are an almost infinite number of ways to do different tasks, any number of ways to get it right. There are also, unfortunately, an almost infinite number of ways to get it wrong – *badly* wrong, in some cases. Which is what the lists of 'warning signs' in each mode are about. And if we don't pay attention to those warning-signs… well, we'd be likely spiral down into some serious sins of dubious discipline. More about those in the next section, then…

SEVEN SINS OF DUBIOUS DISCIPLINE

Before we can put all this into practice, there are a bunch of problems that really *must* be faced. We're aware that we might be a bit unpopular with some folks for saying this, because a few deeply-cherished delusions may get trodden on in the process. But fact is that if we dowsers don't face those delusions... well, to be blunt, there won't be any point in *anything* that's done in dowsing. Yes, it really *is* that bad. Seriously.

The problems range across the full range of quality-issues we've seen earlier, but for convenience, we've clustered them here into what might be called the Seven Sins of Dubious Discipline.

The hype hubris

Sin #1 arises from what we might, in our more polite moments, describe as a triumph of marketing over technical expertise. (There are some other epithets for this that are rather ruder, if often rather more accurate.) Dowsing, earth-mysteries, in fact pretty much every field of study with a strong subjective element, are all plagued by a relentless pursuit of hyped-up glamour – Egypt! Atlantis! the Golden Age! – in which style takes priority over substance. "Never mind the quality, feel the width!", to quote the tag-line from an old TV comedy...

Glamour sells, but it isn't real. Like junk-food advertising, it promises sustenance, but never really delivers, leaving us unsatisfied and wanting more. Yet because the hype seems to be all that's on offer – or at least all that's easily available – we can get sucked back into it, again and again. More to the point, *we* trick ourselves into falling for it, time after time after time. And it's our responsibility to learn to *not* do so – to recognise the hype for what it is, and move on.

> A friend of ours has a habit of visiting a certain fast-food franchise once every few weeks or so. He complains every time about the difference between the glossy airbrushed adverts and the grey flabby vapidity of the real 'un-food'. The resultant stomach-ache can last for days, he says.
>
> He insists he only goes there to remind himself of why he doesn't go there. He hasn't yet noticed that he does indeed go there – time and time again...

Fair enough, the hype and the glamour are often the 'hooks' that grab our attention in the first place, gaining our interest enough to get us started. But at some point – and preferably sooner rather than later – we need to wean ourselves off the pre-digested junk-food, and get down to the real meat of the matter.

It's not just the quality of our own work that's at risk here, because there's also a darker side to this. It's not only that those who do the 'boring' detail-work, often for decades, have no way to publish their results: we've seen all too many cases where they've been misused, plagiarised, derided, then ignored, in a subtle yet sin-gularly nasty form of 'life-theft'. When rip-off artists are rewarded handsomely for taking us all for a ride, whilst 'the little people' who've been stolen from are actively penalised, there's no incentive to do real work. When hype is allowed to masquerade as reality, quality suffers, for *everyone*.

In short, to use the old advertising metaphor, the sizzle ain't the sausage: the hype can sometimes have a useful role to play, but in itself it isn't real. So when someone tries to sell you the sizzle, look for the sausage: if the substance isn't there, it's time to walk away.

Arises from:

- blurring between Artist exuberance and Mystic belief / belonging

Resolve by:

- go to Scientist mode to check facts and sources
- cross-check in Magician mode by questing and testing usefulness of the ideas and assertions

The Golden-Age game

Sin #2 has its source in what we might call 'a bizarre blend of super-science and super-religion'. The idea is that somewhere in the distant past – you pick when and where, there's plenty to choose from – there was just one culture, one civilisation, one faith or whatever, with a special elite class of priest-scientists, separate from mere ordinary mortals, who somehow 'knew it all'. They'd created the perfect utopia, which is ready and waiting for us now, if only we can find the way…

It's a lovely dream, perhaps. Yet that's *all* it is: a lovely dream. And in most cases its hidden purpose is to distract attention from our real responsibilities in the here-and-now. Which is why, if we're not careful, chasing that dream can become a serious sin…

There's no doubt that there *is* value in the quest for the 'Golden Age'. The hope that there can even be such a place – either in the outer world, or within ourselves – is a crucial, essential driver for personal and social change. Yet we need to balance that quest with realism, and with a great deal more honesty and self-honesty than the hype-ridden hagiography of this field will usually allow.

> We were at a conference in Glastonbury – where else? – where we'd been presenting our concerns on this issue. A well-dressed, middle-aged man came up to us afterwards, exuding self-confidence. "You're quite wrong, of course", he boomed, in the rolling, unctuous tones of the much-practised orator, "We know *everything* about Atlantis and the Golden Age. It's all in the ancient Hittite scrolls." A perfectly-timed pause. "Though only the Great Masters can read them, of course." He offered us an indulgent, supercilious smile, turned, and walked away.
>
> We both sighed, releasing a breath that neither of us knew we'd held, and glanced at each other with stunned expressions on our faces. "I rest my case, perhaps…?"

What's going on here is indeed about 'super-science and super-religion' – or more accurately a muddled blurring between the modes of the Scientist and the Mystic. The latter needs, above all, to *believe* in something, deeply, passionately: that's its role. The Scientist needs concrete facts: that's its role, too. But in the Golden Age Game, beliefs are treated as fact, and facts are filtered to fit in with the assumptions of the belief. Neither mode is used correctly; and whenever any kind of challenge occurs in one mode, the game jumps across to the other mode *whilst still purporting to use the first mode's rules*. It is fact because I believe it to be true; since it is fact, it is therefore true, hence must be believed by all. Round and round the garden we go: no checks, no balances, no questions – and no question of *usefulness*, either. And behind it, all too often, a subtle unacknowledged arrogance: we followers of the Golden Age are also, by definition, members of that special elite, the 'Chosen Ones', whilst all other 'unbelievers' are not...

When we *do* check those claims against real-world analogues, such as Australian aboriginals, or the Amazonian peoples, it's true we do often find a deep knowledge that can be far outside of what's known in mainstream 'techno-scientific' culture – which is why drug-companies and others fund expeditions to raid and, bluntly, steal as much of that knowledge as they can. Yet that knowledge is also highly *contextual* – in other words, it lives as much in the Magician mode as the Scientist or Mystic – and always derives in part from the *personal* experience of the Artist mode. And though the respective lore may well have been passed down through an unbroken line of elders or grandmothers – who may well guard that knowledge with care, for reasons of health and safety if nothing else - there's no real evidence for anything resembling the Golden Age's beloved priesthood-elites. Just ordinary people, living their lives in their own particular way, with their own particular, peculiar responsibilities. Just like us, in fact.

The 'truths' of the Scientist and Mystic have no meaning on their own – and especially not when they're mangled in Golden Age myths. To reach anything that anyone can use, they need to be balanced with the Magician's awareness of appropriateness. And as dowsers we can also use the Artist mode to find more from the landscape than could be learned from a half-imaginary translation of some half-invented 'ancient scroll'.

So whilst no dowser would doubt that there are real mysteries yet to be explored, the Golden-Age Game *distracts* from that deeper exploration. Its purported marvels consist of little more than a handful of mysteries taken far out of their real context, contorted by clueless 'cultural imperialism', narcissistic nostalgia and self-centred delusions of grandeur, and blown up out of all proportion by wishful thinking, hype and hope.

More than hope, perhaps. There's a Welsh word 'hiraedd' that describes this well: woefully mistranslated as 'homesickness', it's more "a longing and grieving for that which is not, has never been and can never be". We do need to respect that grief: when we look deeply into it, it hurts more than most can bear. Yet building Golden-Age myths to hide from the hurt just does not help. Take that alone-ness, that crushing sadness, and work *with* it to build something real instead.

There *is* nowhere else, no-when else to which we can run away from the perils and problems of the present. If it can be said to exist at all, the only possible Golden Age we can experience exists in what *we* create, here, and now

Arises from:

- blurring between Mystic mode (belief, and desire for sense of belonging to something 'special and different') and Scientist mode (beliefs mistaken for facts)

Resolve by:

- maintain clear distinction between Mystic and Scientist
- balance with Magician and Artist modes to establish context, meaning and use

The newage nuisance

Sin #3 is perhaps more subtle, yet certainly no less of a problem in practice, because where the Golden Age Game is careless in its use of the Scientist and Mystic modes, the Newage Nuisance plays fast and loose with them all...

Although it can take almost any form, in essence it's a dilettante 'disneyfication' of discipline itself – a shallow over-simplification of everything, combined with a wilful, sometimes deliberate and often near-obsessive *avoidance* of any kind of discipline. The term 'newage' rhymes with 'sewage', 'the discarded remnant of what was once nutritious' – and its stench pervades pretty much every area that purports to be 'New Age'.

To be fair, the problem isn't unique to the New Age – we've also seen it occur everywhere from information-system design to intellectual-property law, from economics to ecofeminism, and almost anything in

Though there are some strong links with Sin #7, inadequate management of the skills-learning process (see *Lost in the learning labyrinth*, p.87), newage is typified by arbitrary jumps between the distinct forms of 'truth' in art, spirituality, science and magic. At its simplest and most forgivable level, it'll often occur when an overdose of enthusiasm overrides sense and self-honesty – such as in the feeling of 'instant mastery' after the classic New Age-style one-weekend-workshop.

The excessive exuberance of 'beginner's luck' is understandable, but the real problems start whenever there's an unwillingness, or refusal, or fear, to let go of that feeling of 'instant mastery'. So the next stage is the 'workshop junkie' – a ceaseless collection of just the 'instant mastery' level of every possible new skill, but with no depth, no commitment, and nothing to tie the skills together into anything that can be put to practical use.

> One of our 'witchy' friends unwittingly illustrated this for us the other day. "We go to one workshop after another", she wailed. "We get meaning, fun, togetherness, one revelation after another. But what do we *do* with all this stuff?'"

Part of the problem - especially in New Age contexts with an overt emphasis on 'spirituality' – is that the Mystic mode is all about *being*, about inner-truth: it's diametrically opposed to the Magician mode, which happens to be the only place where "what do we *do* with all this stuff?" comes into the picture. But the real core is that commitment to the discipline of a skill is what finally kills off beginner's luck, and with it that initial delusion of 'mastery'. From there on, for quite a long while, it *feels* like downhill all the way – and hard work too, with personal challenges that are often far harder still. An uncomfortable time, to say the least.

So there's a natural tendency to try to avoid that discomfort by avoiding commitment, whilst still pretending – if only to self – that mastery has already been achieved. There's then an inevitable desire to conceal – if only from self – the fact that mastery has *not* been reached... And the mechanism to do this is by playing mix-and-match between the modes: the rules of one mode are used to validate the 'truths' from another.

The simplest and perhaps most common example of this is actually nowhere near the New Age at all, but in the phrase 'applied science'. *Doing* anything, *using* anything, places us in the

Magician mode of outer-value, and must always be tested in those terms – such as ethics, appropriateness and so on. But the phrase 'applied science' implies that if we can call something 'scientific', the only test we need apply is outer-truth – which means it's 'value-free'. If something's supposedly value-free, that absolves us from having to face any difficult doubts about ethics or effectiveness: so we then claim an unquestioned right to go right ahead and do whatever-it-is *because* it's 'true'. Therein lie all manner of *interesting* problems in the wider world…

Looking at the paths between the modes, you'll see there's at least a dozen different ways this game can go. For example, for dowsers and others whose work is anchored more in the subjective space, one such mistake is typified by a common misuse of the old slogan 'the personal is political': "this is true for me, therefore it must also apply to everyone else", muddling the subjective space ('personal') with the objective space ('political'). The *only* way we can resolve the Newage Nuisance is to be clear about which mode we're in at all times, using the correct rules for that mode, and that mode alone – and also face the fears that drive us to be dishonest about what our skills really are.

> There can be a lot of emotion tied up in that self-dishonesty, so a common characteristic in some forms of the Newage Nuisance is an odd kind of bullying bluster – especially in response to anything that could be construed as critique.
>
> One example we remember well was an ecofeminist artist and writer whose work we'd much admired, until a feminist academic pointed out to us that her supposed studies on 'women's myths and secrets' would best described as "all the fact that's fit to invent" – most of her assertions had no historical basis at all. We should perhaps also have noticed rather earlier her penchant for using 'patriarchy' as an all-purpose synonym for 'bad' – other-blame being another common characteristic of this kind of newage. With some trepidation, we asked her about her sources.
>
> "Myself, of course! – my own experience of the patriarchy's oppression of women!"
>
> "But you're presenting it as objective fact?"
>
> "It's true because I *feel* it to be true. So it's true for all women!"
>
> "But if you're presenting it as fact, surely it needs to follow a science-style discipline of cross-references and so on?"
>
> "It's women's spirituality! Science doesn't apply – that's just the patriarchy!"
>
> "But what spiritual discipline do you use?"

> "It's *art* – you can't question *that*!", she snapped, with something close to a sneer.
>
> "But you're insisting that other women must *do* things your way, to base their own lives on these personal experiences of yours – how is that art?"
>
> "Because it's *true*! *Everything* I say is true! If you doubt that, you're just an agent of the patriarchy – the *enemy*!"
>
> Round and round the garden... Yup, we kinda gave up at that point...
>
> Kind of reminded us of some of the dowsers we knew, too. Ourselves as well at times, to be honest. Oops...

The Newage Nuisance is the Golden Age Game writ large, covering the entire context of the space in which we work. Challenging it is never easy, given the emotions that such challenges will so often engender. Yet unless we do each face it firmly – not just in others, but even more in ourselves, in everything *we* do – that avoidance of discipline will *inevitably* render meaningless every scrap of work in that space.

Not exactly a trivial sin, then. One we *definitely* need to address...

Arises from:

- combination of incompetence and self-dishonesty in relation to any or all of the modes, and fear of responsibilities from commitment to a skill

Resolve by:

- be clear which mode we're in at each moment, and use *only* the rules and tests for that specific mode
- be clear how and why we transition from mode to mode
- challenge and face the fears that would otherwise lead to evasion of the necessary discipline in each mode

The meaning mistake

Sin #4 occurs mainly in and around the Scientist mode, where we aim to establish outer-truth, otherwise known as 'fact'. There are clear rules in this mode for deriving fact; the Meaning Mistake occurs whenever we've been careless with those rules, leading us to think we've established that 'truth' when we haven't.

The simplest way to describe this is with a cooking metaphor: the end-results of our tests for meaning should be properly cooked, but if we're not careful, they'll end up half-baked, overcooked, or just plain inedible.

Interpretations go *half-baked* when we take ideas or information out of one context, and apply them to another without considering the implications of doing so. One form of this is what scientists describe as 'induction', or reasoning from the particular to the general – as in that misuse of the feminist slogan "the personal is political", where we assume that whatever happens to us must also apply to everyone else. We then leap to conclusions without establishing the foundations for doing so – which can cause serious problems when we try to apply them in practice in the Magician mode.

> 'Half-bakery' is a common characteristic of newage, but it occurs often enough in the sciences too. A classic example in archaeology is RJC Atkinson's infamous 'reconstruction' of how the bluestones were brought by sea from the Prescelly mountains in Wales to Stonehenge. Alan Sorrell's drawings for Atkinson show wild savages propelling a raft with makeshift paddles and a wind-tattered sail – and the four-ton bluestone lashed *on top* of the raft.
>
> Atkinson was a competent archaeologist, but clearly knew nothing about boats – the whole thing is best described as 'suicide by sea'. You could just about get away with it on a placid inland river, but offshore the first real wave would flip the whole thing over, drowning everyone on board. As maverick archaeologist Tom Lethbridge pointed out, a more viable solution would be to sling the stone *underwater*, as a stabilising keel between two sea-going canoes – as he'd seen Eskimoes do in the Arctic.

Perhaps a better dowsing example would be the use of terms such as 'frequency', 'vibration', 'radiation' or 'energy' – each of which has a precise meaning in science, but in dowsing is often no more than a fairly loose metaphor. The catch is that as a metaphor, it has no definitions on which to anchor either itself or any cross-references. So if we then take the metaphor too literally – the 'frequency' of an imagined 'vibration', perhaps – we soon end up with something that's meaningless to anyone else, and probably to ourselves as well. The moves towards standardised definitions in dowsing do help – such as the Earth Energies Group's *Encyclopaedia of Terms* – but there's no means to define meaningful values for frequencies and the like when the only possible standards reside in people's heads. There doesn't seem to be any way round this problem, either. Tricky…

Interpretations risk going *overcooked* whenever we skip a step in the tests, or ignore warnings from the context that we're looking in the wrong way or at the wrong place. It's the right overall approach – deduction, or reasoning from the general to the particular, rather than induction – but even a single missed step can soon take the reasoning so far sideways as to invalidate the lot.

> One of the classic clues that's something's gone overcooked is the phrase "must be…".
>
> Some years back the physicist John Taylor became interested in dowsing, and decided to do some tests, looking for '*the* mechanism' by which it worked. We could have told him beforehand this was not a good idea – other physicists over the past century or so have shown that many different mechanisms can be involved, and can switch between them almost at random. But no matter, at least he started the right way, by going back to first principles. "There are only four forces in the universe", he asserted: "weak nuclear, strong nuclear, electromagnetic, gravitational. It *must be* one of those."
>
> So far so good, sort of. But then his scientific certainty got the better of him: "It *must be* electromagnetic, and it *must be* in this frequency band." By then the smell of burning was beginning to be noticeable to everyone – yet still Taylor kept going. "I couldn't find any effect in that band", he said, "therefore it *must be* that dowsing does not exist."
>
> To those who don't know how science works, that chain of reasoning might at first seem to make sense: but in fact it's so overcooked as to be charcoaled toast. And when even the normally staid journal *New Scientist* hauled him over the coals for it, so was Taylor's reputation…

Deduction works by narrowing scope, narrowing the range of choices. In formal scientific experimentation, we're supposed to change only one parameter at a time, to ensure that we don't accidentally skip a step and narrow the scope inappropriately. But if we don't know what all the parameters are, it's all too easy to change more than one as we change the conditions of the experiment. A lot more than one parameter, sometimes… And as soon as we do so, we go overcooked.

> The problem here is that it's very easy to go overcooked without realising it: one missed check that we didn't even know we needed can ruin the whole dish.
>
> At Belas Knap we'd been doing some experiments to check for possible sources of very low-frequency sound, using a home-built detector constructed by an engineer friend. This was strict physics – no dowsing involved in this case – but still looking for 'earth mysteries'-type anomalies. The sensor had a microphone at one end of the box, with a loudspeaker on the side to give an audible signal.

> The first time we used the box, we thought we'd found a consistent effect, very similar to the 'bands' often found by dowsing on standing-stones and the like. The speaker was quiet at ground-level, but went louder about six inches above the ground, then quiet again a bit higher, and so on – a repeating pattern. *Very* exciting – we demonstrated it to some visitors at the site, too.
>
> But when we talked it through with the engineer, he couldn't make sense of it: the sensor hadn't been designed to work that way at all. Then a horrid realisation, followed by some quick calculations, and crestfallen faces all round his workbench. The pitch of the sound from the speaker had the exact same wavelength – distance from peak to peak – as the pattern we'd found. So it was just a feedback effect between speaker and microphone – nothing to do with the site at all. We'd gone overcooked, but didn't know it, because we hadn't known till then how the sensor worked.
>
> Embarrassing, to say the least, given how we'd hyped it up to those visitors. Oh well, back to the drawing-board…
>
> (As it happens, we *did* get some real results in the end, but that's another story…)

For dowsers, one essential defence against overcooking is to include an 'Idiot' response in the instrument's vocabulary. By that, as we described back in *Know your instrument* (p.8), we mean some kind of dowsing-response that is different to those for neutral, Yes, No, or any of the directional responses, and which indicates that the dowsing-question – whatever it is – can't be answered in any meaningful way by Yes or No or suchlike. "Un-ask the question" is what the 'Idiot' response really means.

To give a really simple example, how would your pendulum respond to a double-question such as "Should I go left or right?", or a double-negative such as "Is this not the right way to go?" The pendulum's usual yes-or-no answers can't make any sense here – so you'll *need* another kind of response to warn you of that. That type of response is also helpful in providing feedback to improve the skill in developing questions that *can* be answered meaningfully just by Yes or No – and as any scientist knows, the hardest part of the discipline is designing the right questions for an experiment to answer.

So if we're not careful, we can find ourselves in the half-bakery, or with our questing overcooked. Worse, we can easily do both at once – which gives results that really are *inedible*. Courtesy of the Newage Nuisance, the New Age fields are riddled with it – and it doesn't exactly help that the incompetence is then glossed over with hype (Sin #1) or some kind of golden-age myth (Sin #2).

Sadly, the dowsing disciplines can be far from immune from this problem, too.

> One example we often quote was an Australian who insisted that dowsing was strictly about *physical* radiations – which, bluntly, we know it isn't: He had some strange ideas about limits, too: only certain special people – those without fillings or scars or glasses – could use the "radial detector, *miscalled* the divining rod", he thundered.
>
> Some years later, he came across map-dowsing – but still desperately clung to his assertion that it worked only with physical radiations. The place somehow 'knew' that it had to send these radiations to every map and photograph of itself, he said – even a hand-drawn sketch-map. Which stretches credibility a bit, to say the least. And by the time he'd insisted that such dowsing could be done only at midnight, beneath a bare electric light-bulb, by a person who must have no clothes on, it was clear that he'd lost the plot completely. Might have worked for him that way, perhaps – but most of us find simpler ways to do it...

One useful hint comes from what Edward de Bono describes as his 'First Law of Thinking': "proof is often no more than a lack of imagination". (There's also a rather more forceful version which asserts that "certainty comes only from a feeble imagination"...) The problem here is that, in itself, the Scientist mode doesn't *have* any imagination: it just follows the rules. So we need to be able to dive into one of the 'value' modes – usually the Artist, but also the Magician – to collect new ideas to play with, and bring them back for the Scientist to test. We do have to remember to distinguish between the new ideas – the imagination – and facts – the results of tests – but with care it does work well. This is just as true in the sciences, too: Beveridge's classic *The Art of Scientific Investigation* talks about the use of chance, of intuition, of dreams, and the hazards and limitations of reason – "the origin of discoveries is beyond the reach of reason", he says.

What won't help here is the Mystic mode: in fact it can *cause* the Meaning Mistake, because it treats its beliefs *as* facts – taking them as true 'on faith', so to speak. Muddled ideas about 'spirituality' can easily lead to the Newage Nuisance; but when self-styled 'scientists' start treating their beliefs as fact, they end up with a bizarre, aggressive pseudo-religion called 'scientism' that can be a real nuisance for anyone working in the subjective space.

> For dowsers, one infamous example of scientism at its worst is in the antics of the Skeptics Society, and in particular, their so-called 'Skeptics Challenge'.
>
> The Challenge is a popular means for the Skeptics to harass country dowsers, though the overall aim is to discredit dowsing in general. It's

typically set up at a country fair somewhere – we've come across it in Britain, Australia and the US, and heard of it in other countries too. They lay out a marked-out arena with buried bottles of water, and ask the general public to use dowsing rods to try to find them. They then record the results – and publish them with glee, because whilst the untrained public tend to perform pretty much to chance, professional water-finders tend to be quite a lot *less* 'successful' at finding the buried bottles. This, say Skeptics, *proves* that dowsing is a fraud.

Sure, it all *looks* scientific: but in reality it is, at best, scientific incompetence on the Skeptics' part – completely inedible, in terms of the Meaning Mistake. The chance-figures for the general public are fair enough under the circumstances; but those for the dowsers are not. *At all*. Unfortunately it does take some knowledge of science to see how the game is rigged against any real dowser – and the Skeptics seem to be banking that most people won't know this.

For a start, it's a poorly-designed experiment. Not only does the Challenge take no account of the 'equation of need', but professional water-finders spend their working lives looking for significant quantities of *flowing* water far below ground – and in most cases would aim to filter out from their awareness anything as insignificant as a small static bottle close to the surface. In that sense, the experiment-design itself is at fault: it doesn't test real-world conditions. In fact it looks suspiciously like it's *designed* to fail – which really *would* be scientific fraud...

And in terms of statistics, the below-chance figure for the professionals does *not* prove that they're worse than the general public, as Skeptics have claimed. *Any* significant deviation – positive *or* negative – indicates a significant effect: and a negative deviation usually indicates a fault in experiment-design. In this case, what it really indicates is either that the Skeptics who designed the Challenge have a very poor understanding of science and statistics, or else they're playing dirty, and know it. We have our suspicions, but we'd better give them the benefit of the doubt...

Either way, the Skeptics Challenge is no true challenge at all: something that dowsers need to be aware of, and avoid.

As with the 'must-be mistake', another warning-sign of potential inedibility is any use of a phrase such as "it's obvious" or "of course it's the same as..." – because they usually mean that a key step or test has been skipped ('obvious'), or a simile has been mistaken for fact.

But the only true protection against the Meaning Mistake is to recognise that the Scientist mode has strict rules for meaning, to derive what it calls 'fact' – and we cannot be careless with those rules if we want our work to be meaningful in that mode. We can go off briefly to other modes to gather new ideas to test: but in the

Scientist mode itself, there's no middle ground – either something is fact, or it isn't.

Arises from:

- carelessness with the rules for the Scientist mode
- blurring with the Mystic mode by treating 'scientific' beliefs as fact

Resolve by:

- watch carefully for keyphrases such as "of course" or "it's obvious" or "must be", all of which indicate a high probability of meaning-mistakes
- in dowsing, include an 'Idiot' or 'un-ask the question' response in the vocabulary to reduce the risk of overcook

The possession problem

Sin #5 is somewhat different from the others, because it doesn't arise from mistakes with the modes as such, but from another source entirely: ego. And behind that, all too often, are un-acknowledged fears that can be surprisingly hard to face...

In essence, the problem is a fear of uncertainty. When the world becomes too complex for comfort, there's a natural tendency to cling on to what we know, what we have, what we believe, and claim exclusive ownership of all such things. In short, the problem is one of possession – but in both senses of the word, both possess*ing* and possess*ed*. In our context here, we see this most often in two different forms:

- possession as separation – for example, the concept of a 'sacred site' as something separate from the rest of the landscape
- possession as possessing 'the truth' – evidenced in 'religious wars' such as the Skeptics' tirades against dowsers and others, or 'mainstream' versus 'alternative' approaches to healing

The first trap is that neither places nor ideas are commodities to be possessed: they simply *are*. And whilst a notion of stewardship does work as a model for ownership of such things, possession doesn't: it gets in the way, all the time.

> Perhaps off-topic, we admit, but if you're interested in how the issues of the Possession Problem pan out in business and the wider society, see Tom's book *Power and Response-ability: the human side of systems*.

The problem stems in part from a misuse of the Mystic mode. Like the Scientist, the Mystic needs certainty in the form of what it calls 'truth'. But whilst the Scientist gets there by testing and cross-linking everything to everything else, the Mystic simply *declares* something to be 'the truth' – hence 'to take it on faith'. To get round the problem that some things will inevitably not fit with that 'truth', the Mystic mode again simply declares that anything that doesn't fit is 'not-true', to be ignored. It then places an explicit *yet arbitrary* boundary between them: hence, for example, the arbitrary separation between the 'sacred' and the 'profane' – literally 'pro-fanum', 'that which is outside the temple'.

Nothing wrong with that in itself – it's a useful tactic, as we've seen. The problem comes when people think that the boundary is real, that the boundary itself is 'the truth' – and try to possess everything inside it. The amount of emotion unleashed against 'heresy' – which literally translates as nothing more serious than 'to think different' – gives us a rather strong clue that it's not just about 'truth' here… Trying to possess the belief, people end up being possessed by it – which is *not* a good idea.

> The 'must-be mistake' that we saw in Sin #4 can likewise be a problem here, because it's also an attempt to claim a kind of possession of 'the *only* truth'.
>
> For example, the illusionist James Randi, one of the leading lights of the Skeptics Society, has on occasion claimed that if he can reproduce some supposed 'supernatural' event by illusionist means, then that *must be* the way it was done. He appears to believe that this gives him an inalienable right to harass and 'expose' all others as purported frauds.
>
> Somehow it never seems to occur to him that any mechanism other than illusion could possibly be involved. To him, it seems, illusion is the only truth, with himself as its only guardian…
>
> Yet not only is this poor science – the Meaning Mistake – but it's also extraordinarily abusive. As with the Newage Nuisance, this kind of bullying bluster is another all too common characteristic of the Possession Problem.

We've seen some of this already in the Newage Nuisance and Golden-Age Game, of course, but what makes it even messier here is the creation of boundaries that are put up to protect the 'possession'. Reality as a whole doesn't *have* boundaries: pollution takes no notice of national borders, for example. And as dowsers it's not just the fences and walls that get in our way when we're tracking a line – it's the arbitrary *separation* of things that's the real problem, because it prevents us from gaining any sense of the whole.

> Take the example of archaeoastronomy at a site such as the Castlerigg stone circle.
>
> The circle itself is a kind of local focus – the foresight, so to speak – for all the sight-lines that pick out the rise and set positions of sun and moon and stars in that epoch several thousand years ago.
>
> But the other ends of each of the lines – the backsights – are the peaks and notches in the mountains all round the circle, miles away into the distance. The central 'sacred site' makes no sense unless we consider the entire landscape – circles, hills, valleys, mountains, everything – to be part of the site as a whole.

So although it's true that there are places that act as focal-points in some sense or other, there *are* no 'sacred sites' as such – *everywhere* is 'sacred' to someone, in some context. It's all one continuum: creating arbitrary boundaries between the 'sacred' and the 'profane', the 'important' and the 'unimportant', will just get in the way, not only of action, but of thinking, too.

In much the same sense, ideas or theories about the past can become boundaries to our thinking, preventing us from seeing a context in any other way. 'The past' is subjective, not objective: we can't go there, and there's very little that we can test in the Scientist sense – we have no way to tell for certain what people thought, how they felt, what they believed. In a very literal sense, the past is a different country: they did indeed do things differently there, and often for very different reasons than those that would apply in the present time.

So discoveries in the present do not necessarily 'prove' anything about the past. We may well find interesting energies at so-called sacred-sites; we may well find extraordinary astronomical alignments and so on; yet that does *not* mean that any of it was planned by the purported 'astronomer-priests' of the Golden-Age Game. Instead, from what little we know of the cultures concerned, and from equivalent cultures in the present, it seems more likely that such things arose more from the intuition of the Artist – simply, that 'it seemed like a good idea at the time', and was. It's perhaps more useful, too, to apply the Magician's perspective – to ask "what *use* is it?" – than to fight over 'truths' that probably never existed in the first place...

There's also an academic discipline called 'deconstruction' that can be useful here. Its task is to pick apart each assertion of 'truth', so as to surface any hidden assumptions. (Dowsers know all too well the need for this, in designing questions that can be answered meaningfully by a limited set of dowsing-responses – usually just Yes or No.) More useful still is an expanded variant called 'causal layered analysis' which applies the same questioning up and down the layers, from the everyday 'litany of complaint' down to the deep myths and core-beliefs. The aim in both cases is to identify notions and worldviews that are somehow 'privileged' – assumed to be fact, but without any actual questioning to verify it *as* fact.

> One catch to watch here is that the same deconstruction must *always* be applied to the analysis itself, to check for our own hidden assumptions in the way we do it. Kind of mind-bending in its recursion, perhaps, and often personally challenging, too, but it's something that *must* be done if the analysis is to be meaningful.
>
> If we avoid this check, our own worldview becomes 'privileged' – presented as indubitable 'fact', in the classic Possession Problem style – but we have no way to recognise that we've done so. The result is usually some pointless exercise in arrogant 'other-blame', with nothing useful that can be achieved at the end of it.
>
> We've come across this misuse of deconstruction often in some styles of social and environmental activism, for example, though it's also common – if in less overt forms – in much 'New Age' thinking too.

It then becomes useful – if sometimes embarrassing – to ask what worldviews and assumptions tend to be 'privileged' in dowsing, in earth-mysteries and in the 'alternative' fields in general. The Golden-Age Game is one obvious example, but there are plenty of others – such as the tendency to regard anything supposedly 'alternative' as inherently better than anything 'mainstream'.

So another potent source for the Possession Problem is that, in part because of the nature of the Mystic mode, each group and enclave will tend to create, and enforce, its own orthodoxy, its own 'official version' of 'the truth' – frequently deriding anything and anyone else as 'the lunatic fringe'. Archaeology has a long history of this, for example; likewise medicine, in fact pretty much every discipline with a strong subjective base which it needs to present as 'the truth'.

What's interesting, too, is the process by which yesterday's 'heresy' so often becomes today's orthodoxy, and onward to tomorrow's passé 'primitive beliefs'. As Thomas Kuhn showed in *The Structure of Scientific Revolutions*, it's something of a truism that science will progress mainly by the death of senior scientists – especially those who've had a huge personal investment in some particular theory, and will permit change only 'over my dead body', in an all too literal sense… In other words, the Possession Problem again.

The best way round this, perhaps, is to take the long view: 'truth' changes over time, but quality is real, and lasts forever. And if anyone tells you they own 'the truth' about anything, be wary: it's almost certainly a problem of possession.

Arises from:

- excess of certainty, or fear of uncertainty, leading to inappropriate use of the Mystic mode

Resolve by:

- balance with the Magician mode concept that beliefs are tools, not absolutes
- also use the Magician mode to ask "what *use* is it?" rather than only "is it true?"
- watch for arbitrary boundaries between 'sacred' and 'profane', between 'mine' and 'not-mine' and so on, and use insights from the Artist mode to create bridges across the boundaries
- use deconstruction and similar tactics to challenge possession in all its forms – especially in yourself

The reality risk

Sin #6 extends the Meaning Mistake in a rather different direction, but in some ways an even more dangerous one. The problem arises from what at first seems an innocuous question: "is it real or imaginary?" But the question in itself indicates that someone doesn't understand what's going on here. In the subjective space – in pretty much *any* space, really – it's not a question of 'real *or* imaginary', but 'real *and* imaginary' – always both, always together. Yet the way some

people approach this issue could best be described as a health-and-safety hazard akin to playing with matches in a firework factory… a sin indeed…

Let's illustrate why that simplistic split of 'real' versus 'imaginary' is nothing like as straightforward as it seems.

Go into subjective space for a while and imagine an orange. A nice, big, juicy orange.

(You can see it, right? And notice *how* you 'see' it – as an image, as words, as an overall impression, or whatever.)

Heft it in your hand: you can feel its weight, its texture, the slight 'give' as you squeeze it.

Notice its subtle scent, and the even more subtle sound it makes as you squeeze it gently in your palm.

Dig your fingers into the surface: notice as you break through the peel the slight mist of juice, the suddenly much stronger scent.

Strip away the peel, noticing the slight sense of acid-attack on fingernail and cuticle as you do so.

Pull out just one imaginary segment, and put it in your mouth. Notice its papery texture on your tongue, the shape, the promise.

Now bite into it – note the *shock* of flavour, sour, sweet, both, the swirl of saliva in your mouth.

All of that you can feel right now, remember now, know now. True, yes?

And yet it's entirely imaginary.

And yet the saliva is real enough; likewise the overall impressions. And were we to measure such things, the sensory sections in your brain would be registering *something* real – though exactly *what*, it might perhaps not be quite so sure…

All imaginary. *And* real. Not one *or* the other, but *both*.

So although that 'and' can get a bit complicated at times, there *is* no 'or' here. *Everything* is real *and* imaginary, all at the same time.

There's a *huge* hazard here – and like every other hazard, we can't evade it simply by pretending that it isn't there. Time and again we see people playing a bizarre yet potentially lethal game, invoking 'energies', getting wildly excited about them, then walking away without doing any kind of 'tidying up', on the assumption that it's perfectly safe to do so because those energies are "only imaginary". That it's nothing like as simple as that is illustrated by the fact that many of the would-be 'earth-healers' we've known have died relatively young, in most cases from some very nasty cancers. Sorry, folks, but this is *not* a New Age game: and the sooner people wake up to this fact, the better for all…

We perhaps need to hammer this point home: *if you imagine something, it's real* – with all of the risks and hazards that that implies.

> Don't allow yourself to get too distracted by notions of 'fact' here – "is it real or not?" – because fact hardly comes into this picture at all. In this context it's all the Artist or the Magician: the two 'truth' modes – the Scientist and the Mystic – can't help us much here, because they don't *have* any imagination, and hence have no clue what to do with it. In other contexts, yes, that lack of imagination is a real strength: here it's not. Much, anyway.

At the personal level, we'll see some of the same concerns as in the Possession Problem: people thinking they possess some idea, some imagining, but end up becoming 'possessed' *by* it, allowing it to drive their life without – though sometimes, powerless, *with* – conscious awareness of what's going on. The magical traditions provide plenty of warnings on the dangers here, and also what to do about them: Dion Fortune's classic *Psychic Self-Defence* may seem a little dated these days, but it's still an essential reference for anyone working in this space.

Perhaps a simpler example, though, is the actor who takes on a character, Method-style, and then can't get *out* of character at the end of the play. Again, the theatre tradition has its own tactics for dealing with this: Keith Johnstone's *Impro* is a useful reference here, particularly the section on Masks and trance. One of his key points, for example, is that it's essential not to treat a Mask as an inanimate object: each will have its own 'vocabulary' of movements and styles and actions which will tend to be taken on by any actor who wears it. In that sense, to work with a Mask, we have to enter into relationship with it – and recognise that in that relationship the Mask has choices too.

Yet *everything* is a Mask, a 'per-sona' – literally 'that through which I sound'. A dowsing-instrument is a Mask: as we've seen, it too will have its own vocabulary of responses, and every experienced dowser will know that sense of needing to be 'in relationship' with the instrument in order to get it to work well. Likewise every place is a Mask, with its own vocabulary, its own expressions, its own choices: and sometimes we can take on those characteristics without being aware that we're doing so.

> A story of Tom's from some years back would illustrate this – and also how scary it can be if it's not managed well.
>
> With a friend, he was visiting a long-barrow in Somerset called Stoney Littleton. It has quite a long stone passage, perhaps forty feet long and

> four feet high, with two cross-chambers and a three-lobed chamber at the end.
>
> He sat down in the central lobe of the end-chamber, feeling for the energies of the place. What he mostly felt was the dampness in the space: nothing much more than that. He meditated for a while, cross-legged under the low lintel of the roof. Still nothing much: no sense of anything happening at all.
>
> He was aroused a few moments later by what sounded like a gasp of shock from his friend, looking towards him from along the passage, at one of the cross-chambers closer to the entrance. Still looking at him, wide-eyed, she backed out into the open.
>
> "Tom, can you come here, please?", she called, in what was clearly a rather shaken voice.
>
> "What's wrong? What's the problem?"
>
> "N-nothing", she answered, "b-but come out, if you would?"
>
> He got up to his feet, scrambled down the passage, out into the open air, stretched his back. Still tense, she looked at him closely, then finally relaxed.
>
> "Good – it *is* you", she said.
>
> "What do you mean?"
>
> "Well, whoever was down there had horns, for a start..."
>
> Since then we've come across several other people who'd had incidents of the same image at Stoney Littleton: it seems to be a real characteristic of the Mask of that place. Perhaps not a good idea to try to invoke it intentionally, though...

What we may perceive as 'imaginary entities' at a place are also just as real – with everything that that implies. Take the example of 'faery': to those of a New Age bent, this will no doubt bring up the cute image of the Cottingley characters, or Findhorn-style devas, flickering energies like little fluttery things at the bottom of the garden. If so, remember also that in the Irish tradition, the fairies standing guard in front of the hollow hills aren't like that at all: they're seven feet tall with, yes, long pointy ears – but also with long pointy teeth. They don't feel pain, it's said – but they're *fascinated* that you do... In short, be *very* careful what you ask for, for you may just get what you ask...

The same applies with the rather more active 'energies' that can be associated with some types of site. Referred to as 'guardians', they've even been known to follow people home, so to speak, in some cases causing absolute havoc with poltergeist-type effects, or worse. The archaeologist Dr Anne Ross has described one such incident, for example, which was linked to some ancient stone heads she'd found during a dig near Hexham in Yorkshire: the results were very disturbing for all concerned, and it took a lot of work – including a full-blown exorcism – before the incursions ended and were put to rest. So yes, all imaginary, it seems – yet also all too real, in a functional and even physical sense.

Legends and so on will often warn us of potential risks at a place: we need to be aware of this, respect it, and take appropriate action or apply appropriate protection where necessary. As dowsers we should also make use of those 'side-feelings' from the Artist mode to warn us of risks arising whilst we're working: if we get a sudden sense that we should stop working, it's best to do just that, and quickly. And for the same reason it's wise to take a leaf out of the Magician's book, and formally 'close the site' after a session: to quote an old science joke, "please leave this decontamination room as you would wish to find it!"

In this kind of context, 'sins' such as the Hype Hubris, the Golden-Age Game and the Newage Nuisance are not just a problem: they can be downright dangerous for everyone concerned. On the one side, people can become so deluded in their own self-importance that they can be blithely unaware of the real risks involved in these fields; on the other, there can be a fall back to uncontrolled panic when reality finally breaks through. It's not a pretty picture: once again, as with every other skill in a hazard-laden space, this is not a place where childish minds can be let loose to play…

Perhaps the safest approach here would be a Fortean one. Way back at the turn of the previous century, Charles Fort was a journalist who collected information about events that didn't fit with anyone's theories – 'the book of the damned', he called it. Present-day Forteans follow a similar line, yet extend it with a demanding discipline: they document every description of each incident of 'the damned' – fairies, flying saucers, showers of frogs and fishes, you name it – exactly at face-value; but they *don't* interpret. In other words, they keep it strictly in the Artist and Magician modes; the Scientist and the Mystic can perhaps come in later, but they don't belong at all in that early exploratory stage. They work *with* the weird intersection of the imaginary and the real, accepting it for what it is – and reduce the risks accordingly.

Whichever way we look at it, the real is imaginary; the imaginary is real. If you ever forget that fact, you may be putting yourself – and others – at very real risk. You have been warned!

Arises from:

- failure to grasp the deeper complexities – and dangers – of the subjective space

Resolve by:

- reduce the risk with a Fortean approach, recognising that everything is real *and* imaginary at the same time
- recognise the hazards, and use safety-procedures such as the 'can I? may I? am I ready?' checklist, or the magical-tradition ritual of formally opening and closing the circle
- when dowsing, use the 'side-feelings' to warn of potential dangers, or changes that imply that something may be at risk

Lost in the learning labyrinth

Sin #7 doesn't come from misuse of the modes, but mistakes in the skills-learning process – and all of these mistakes are illustrated well in the labyrinth-model we introduced back in *Round the bend* (p.17). The problem here is that although there's only one path, and may *seem* straightforward enough, it's still all too easy to get lost in the labyrinth...

One of the classic New Age mistakes happens right at the start of the learning-process – confusing 'beginner's luck' with real mastery, as we've seen in Sin #3, the Newage Nuisance. If we look at the labyrinth layout, though, we'll see that this is just the first of three places where anyone on the path will seem to be very close to the centre. The other two are at the beginnings of circuit 4, 'caring', and of circuit 7, 'meditation' – which, in their guise as 'the path of heart' and 'the path of spirit' respectively, are likewise classic sources for New Age delusions of 'instant mastery'. There's only one path through the labyrinth – and we can't skip *any* of it if we want to achieve real mastery of a skill.

We've seen earlier that we start out at 'control' – training, in fact – and that it gets *worse* for quite a while as soon as we make the turn outward to circuit 2, 'self'. Note too that the same pattern repeats further in, with the double-jump from 'survival' to 'caring' to 'meditation', and then back outward again to 'mind' and 'communication', it may seem hard to let go from the sense of quiet certainty at the end of 'meditation' and moving outward to 'mind'.

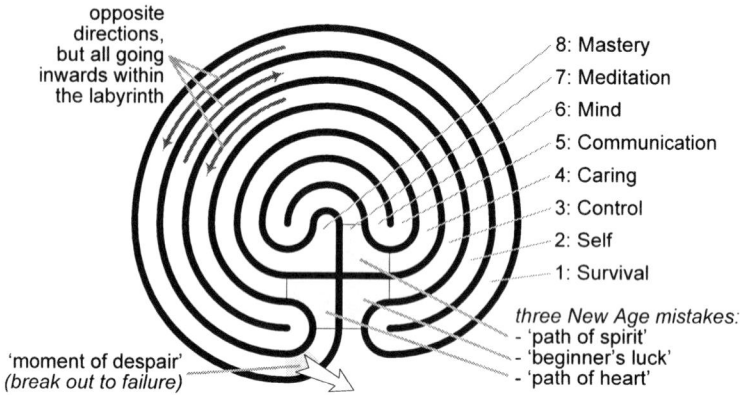

opposite directions, but all going inwards within the labyrinth

8: Mastery
7: Meditation
6: Mind
5: Communication
4: Caring
3: Control
2: Self
1: Survival

three New Age mistakes:
- 'path of spirit'
- 'beginner's luck'
- 'path of heart'

'moment of despair' (break out to failure)

More on the skills-labyrinth

Try tracing the path with your fingertips, from the opening at 'beginner's luck' to the end at 'mastery'. Notice how hard it is to stay on track; notice also the sheer centrifugal force that seems to want to hurl you out of the labyrinth at that bleak moment of despair, at the end of the 'survival' circuit, when you realise that you're not only further out than everyone else in the skill, but worse than when you first started. If you give up at that point, you're likely to lose everything that you've learned; but if you *can* make it round the curve, through the 'dark night of the soul', you'll never lose it – it's that close. (Though notice too that from sheer relief you'll be more prone there to the second of the New Age mistakes, the delusion that the start of the 'path of heart' is the centre – watch out, because there's still a long way to go...)

Another confusion is that 'the dark night of the soul' is the only place in the whole labyrinth where you walk shoulder-to-shoulder with someone else on another circuit who's going the same way. (That the other side of that match is the exuberance of beginner's luck' just makes the agony of the 'dark night' even worse...) Everywhere else in the labyrinth, people going the same way will always seem to be going in opposite directions. Which provides plenty of opportunity for error in the skills-learning process, especially when learning in parallel with others...

So although working on one's own can be lonely, the labyrinth shows there are some subtle problems from working in groups.

Collaboration is important during the later interpretation phase, to build a 'hologram' of the results by viewing the results from many different perspectives. But in the exploratory stage of dowsing fieldwork there can be a real problem of mutual interference from clashing expectations, and from the Possession Problem's all-too-natural tendency to 'help' others by insisting "that's *wrong* – you must do it *this* way!" Not a sin as such, but something of which to be wary.

A final trap is that the whole process is recursive: we're each traversing not just one labyrinth, but an infinite number of them, layers within layers, all at the same time. The moment you hit mastery at one level may well be the same moment that you hit the despair of the 'dark night' on another – and vice versa, of course. There's no avoiding this: you can only win if you commit to the game, and the only escape-route would cause you to lose the lot. So despite the roller-coaster ride, the wild twists and turns, the labyrinth shows there's just one simple way to improve the skill, and the quality of the work. To stay un-lost in the learning-labyrinth, all you have to do is to keep going, keep going, one step at a time.

Arises from:

- failure to understand and accept the process of learning new skills

Resolve by:

- use the labyrinth as a study-guide for potential problems, and act on any issues accordingly

Cleansing the sins

This heading might perhaps sound a bit biblical and blaming, but it's nothing like that bad – honest! The point we're aiming to make here is that what we've shown in the sections above are indeed 'sins', and they do indeed need to 'cleansed' if there's to be any chance of lifting the quality of dowsing practice – but it might first be useful to remember what 'sin' actually *means*…

The literal translation of the word is something like 'error', with an extra emphasis on what would otherwise be called 'ignorance'. So the 'sins' are just errors of practice that need to be fixed, mistakes that anyone can fall into – mistakes that we *all* fall into from time to time, to be honest about it. It's not a big deal. It's just that facing the 'sins' is what will make the difference between work that is meaningless, bluntly, and work that will have real value for you and for everyone else.

So what's the way out? Practice, practice, self-awareness and more practice, would be the real answer – as for every discipline, in fact. Yet there are also a couple of useful hints from the two different meanings of 'ignorance'.

The first is that sense of 'being in ignorance', of not knowing. Well, now you *do* know about each of those Seven Sins, and we've given some suggestions as to how to tackle each of them in practice: so you can't claim you're in ignorance any more, can you? (say we with a bright grin or two!)

The other sense is trickier: that of wilful 'ignore-ance'. If you know about the problems, but deliberately *choose* to ignore them – and ignore the consequences too, in all probability – there'd not be much we could do to help you there. We can warn you about the sins, but we can't cleanse your sins *for* you, y'see...

Your choice: it's *always* your choice. Quality is a *personal* commitment, a *personal* responsibility.

And with that central point, we've really come to the end of all we can show you about the disciplines of dowsing, and about the practical problems of creating quality in the subjective space. All that remains now is to illustrate all of this with some examples of how we ourselves put these principles into practice in our day-to-day dowsing work.

PRACTICE – ENHANCING THE SENSES

Enough of theory – time to get out of the armchair! So much of the dowsing space at present seems to be dominated by conversations over the Net: but whilst talk may be pleasant, on its own it rarely provides anything new. Instead, we need to engage the subtle senses of the Artist mode: and for that, getting our boots muddy, so to speak, is the only way that real change in discipline is likely to happen.

If your interest, like ours, is in archaeology and 'earth-mysteries', that literally means going out and getting your boots muddy: there's a real shift that happens in spending time out in the field, dowsing in any weather, struggling with wind blowing the rods around, and rain down the back of the anorak! Or if your dowsing focus is more on healing and the like, get away from the charts and diagrams and lists for a while: your equivalent of 'fieldwork' would be something like massage, using the fingers and wrists and elbows to sense out the 'musclescape', its folds and curves, its overlays and layers, its smooth flows and locked, tangled places.

In fieldwork, we build relationship with place – whatever 'place' in the respective context might be. A New Age-style quick flit from one site to another won't give space for this: it'd only deliver a few fleeting experiences, perhaps, a few brief encounters with beginner's luck. Perhaps some sort of shallow appreciation over-all, it's true, but not much depth, nothing on which to build a real understanding. From our own experience, reaching for a deeper connection with place is like building a relationship with a skittish horse: there's a crucial change in perspective that starts to settle in after three to six months or so – and that requires patience, a *commitment* to place, in all its modes and moods.

Also crucial is that most of the subtle details are visible only in the field. To see them, we need to develop 'fieldworker's eyes', the fieldworker's senses – and learn *notice* the differences, the edges, the subtle – or not-so-subtle – hints that things have changed.

Many years ago, Tom used to teach dowsing at evening-classes in London. He took one group out on a country field-trip, to practice in a different environment. And there, down a beautiful long avenue, most of the students had found what they were certain was a water-line crossing the road. They called him over to check with his rods, to which he replied "No need, I *know* there's water there."

"How?", they asked. "Have you been here before? What dowsing instrument did you use, to find it from there?"

Smiling, he pointed to his eyes. "Look at the trees", he said. "See what *types* they are: cherry, cherry, cherry, willow, cherry, cherry. Cherry trees hate getting their feet wet; willows love it. Where's the water?"

Intervisibility is another type of connection that can only be identified in the field. At Avebury stone circle, for example, the ancient mound of Silbury Hill is just visible over the skyline: anyone standing on its summit would appear to float between the nearby ridge and the distant hills. More to the point, the notches on its sides, close to the top – which, courtesy of some truly amazing early engineering, have not faded or slumped in several thousand years – line up *exactly* with the line of the intervening ridge. There's no way to identify this from a map, or an air-photograph: you'd have to *be* there to see it.

The same is true of most 'ley-hunting', searching for alignments of ancient sites in the landscape. Anyone can find any number of these with a ruler dropped onto a map – a matter of considerable excitement a few decades ago – but in reality, in most cases, it's probably 'just coincidence'. There *are* real alignments to be found: but they can only be verified by cross-checking the map with what can be seen and felt in the field. John Michell, in his study of ley-type alignments in Land's End at the tip of Cornwall, found that the key standing-stones were each exactly on the skyline from one to the next – yet usually only one could be seen in each direction, on a line 'of rifle-barrel accuracy' over many miles. In a dowsing sense, there's also a distinct 'feel' that goes with an alignment of ancient sites that seems to have been intentional: and one that's not will usually feel 'flat', or 'dead', or simply have no feel at all.

So in fieldwork we need to get out of the usual over-reliance on the head, the intellect, the 'truth' of the Scientist and the Mystic, and instead explore the *feel* of places in their own context. The journey, the process of 'pilgrimage' to the place, often matters as much as the destination. And we need to engage not just our eyes, but sight, sound, scent, taste, touch, synaesthesia – *all* of the senses, all of the elements. Notice the nature of the site itself: slow down to notice the pace of the place, its seasons, its subtleties… moss, plants, water, the sound of wind through the leaves…

butterflies and birds and other small creatures scuttling around in the undergrowth…

Belas Knap forecourt, with dog

It's important, too, to watch for the Mystic mode's tendency to create arbitrary boundaries between things, because they rarely help in the field. One such example is the imagined separation between city and country, and especially the common assumption amongst would-be pagans that 'country is good, city is bad' – because city-spaces do each have their own magic, even if it may be disguised deep beneath detritus, dust and diesel-fumes!

Enjoyment is important, too. Ritual and music and the like can help to engage the senses, but perhaps the wisest way is simply to have *fun* – laughter and merriment do matter! Having fun is also the best way to cope with fieldwork's inevitable chaos… We do need also to watch for the tendency to be over-serious: we need a little craziness to break free of assumptions, and to jiggle the propensity to settle into the ruts of the Meaning Mistake or the Possession Problem.

One such illustration would be the tendency to assess everything in terms of the current *craze du jour*. A decade or two ago it would have been ley-lines, or 'energy leys', whilst a present-day example might be the 'Michael and Mary lines', from Hamish Miller and Paul Broadhurst's book *The Sun and the Serpent*. We've often seen people ask dowsing-questions such as "Are Michael and Mary energies present here?" at every site they've visited – even though Hamish and Paul themselves insist that those terms should only be used in relation to that single landscape-pattern across a single segment of southern England.

We've even seen one book which arbitrarily applies a metaphoric crowbar to the Michael and Mary lines, to force-fit an imagined extension to one of the islands in the Azores. This *proves*, says the author, that this *must be* the original Atlantis – thus combining the

Hype Hubris, the Meaning Mistake and the Golden-Age Game all within one single exercise in absurdity.

Hamish shook his head in wry bemusement when we told him this tale. "It's at least a thousand miles off course", he said, with a sigh. As researchers we can't control others' muddle-headed manglings of our published work, of course, but we do sometimes wish we could!

To break free from the Meaning Mistake – and for that matter the Golden Age Game, or the Newage Nuisance in general – it's essential to be able to go back to first principles, and use the Artist mode to provide hints and suggestions for suitable questions in the respective context.

An example here is a set of megalithic monuments at Meizo, in northern Portugal. At first sight one of the barrows looks like the entrance to a second-world war bunker, with rectilinear slabs of stone forming a zigzag entrance to the underground chamber: but in fact it dates back some six or seven thousand years – almost as old relative to the Stonehenge trilithons as the trilithons are to us.

Meizo dolmen, northern Portugal

What dowsing questions would we use here? We could start with water-lines, perhaps, but even that soon fails to make sense in terms of anything else we know…

Thirty yards away lies another wrecked dolmen. Its 'feel' is completely different, but how would you describe that difference? Feels somehow *wrong*, sad, depressed, even dangerous…? How would you document that difference? – what words or images would you use? Again, what dowsing questions would make sense here? How much use *is* the cut-and-dried yes/no of conventional dowsing in this context?

The 'feel' of a place is often made up of small subtleties that may make no sense at all to anyone else – such as the sudden arrival and disappearance of an inquisitive little lizard from its home inside one of the dolmens at the Meizo site. What is it that makes sense to you? How would you express that sense to others? And in what ways would it matter to do so?

This sense of the importance of small subtleties has been champ-
ioned by the English charity Common Ground. For example, their
Rules for Local Distinctiveness provides a useful checklist to help
open an awareness of these subtleties of place. One such theme
that we've come across before, in the discussion on the Possession
Problem, is that every place is both itself and part of something
greater – a locale, a district, a region of the landscape. Everything
is separate, yet there also *is* no separation: every place contains
within itself every other place.

Another Common Ground theme is to "recognise and respect the
local legends". Every place has its stories, its interweaving of past and
present.

'Wedding Stone', south central Portugal

For example, there's a standing-stone in south central Portugal
nicknamed the 'wedding stone'. It stands about ten feet tall, oddly
shaped like a partly-closed hand. The folklore there is that if you throw
a stone up onto the flat 'fingers', and it stays on top, you'll be married
soon! Yet that story is only two or three hundred years old at most –
whilst the stone itself has probably been there for at least twenty times
as long, from Neolithic times, or even earlier.

In reality, the local legend tells us nothing about why the stone was put
there in the first place. We have no way to know why 'the Ancients'
did as they did in these places – we can only know how *we*, and others,
respond to the Mask of each place in the 'now'.

So history is also now – the *interweaving* of past and present and
future. Everywhere is an interaction between people and place –
and sometimes the place has choices too. Sometimes the interweaving may be uneasy, a somewhat unwilling coexistence, such
as the modern highway that follows the Roman road in bending
around the ancient mound of Silbury Hill. Sometimes the times
can collide, as with the Puritan fanatic 'Stonekiller Robinson', who

set out to destroy all of the megaliths at nearby Avebury, and was almost killed by them instead. But what *doesn't* work is an attempt to 'freeze' time in the present, Heritage-style – because when a place can no longer change, it dies…

Common Ground also warn us that, if we're not careful, we can end up 'loving a site to death'. One example would be the Anta Grande dolmen, near Almendres in central Portugal. As the name suggests, it's *big*: the passage is almost forty feet long, five feet wide, more than six feet high, whilst the inside of the chamber is an astonishing twenty feet high, and the vast mound – what's left of it – is higher still.

Remains of Anta Grande dolmen, Almendres, central Portugal

But after fifty years as an unmanaged tourist-site, it is, bluntly, a wreck: not much litter or graffiti, amazingly, but the passage is blocked with shoring-timbers, one of the main capstones has fallen, another fallen stone almost worn through by the footprints of countless visitors, whilst the whole is covered over by a rickety, rusting tin roof. Too popular. Too many people. Too many un-restored excavations. Ouch.

The same goes for so many places like poor old Stonehenge, of course, with something like a half a million disappointed tourists every year. Avebury is a much larger site, but even that shows many signs of struggling to cope. So we need a bit more discipline in this, too: spread the load among a much wider range of places rather than focussing only on the well-known few.

Might learn a bit more that way, too.

PRACTICE – SETUP AND FIELDWORK

Before we go on to some worked examples, it might be useful to summarise what we actually *do*, before, during and after a field-work session.

Preparation

This may come as a surprise to some, it seems, but it usually *is* a good idea to do at least some preparation before going on-site…

Fair enough, like most people, on occasion we'll somehow just find ourselves at a site, without any real plan of what we'll do, or even much idea of why we're there. But in those cases we'll know to keep it strictly to the Artist mode – or at most a blend of the Artist and the Mystic – and will often leave the dowsing-rods behind. It'll be more about just *being* – the 'doing no-thing' that in Zen Buddhism would be called 'shikan-taza', 'just sitting'.

In most cases, though – particularly if we're working on a longer-term project – we'll have something more definite in mind. Some of the preparation would include:

- what sites do we know which are likely to represent what we're exploring?
- what is already known about the site? – its archaeology, archaeoastronomy, history, usage-patterns, legends, folklore and the like; also previous dowsing and other research, and locations of pipelines, pylons, underground cables and other distractions
- what would be our primary purpose for a session at the site? – examples might include a conventional water-line dowsing-survey, archaeographic analysis of rock-art, a GPS-based sensings-map, watching people's interactions with the site, mapping animal-tracks as non-human interactions with the site, and so on

- what would be our primary mode for the session? – usually just *one* of the Artist, the Mystic, the Magician or the Scientist, with the other modes in support
- what equipment will we need to bring? – dowsing rods, survey gear, record-books, drawing-pads, cameras and other electronics, to name just a few of our routine items
- who would we need to contact for access to the site? – or for any other permissions, such as Heritage or conservation
- what potential hazards exist at the site? – anything from farm-animals to phantoms, from bogs to barbed-wire, from inquisitive tourists to vehicle and equipment security, and so on

We'll also need to consider the *ethics* of what we aim to do. To use the old native American yardstick, we should consider any impacts on at least the next seven generations, and the previous seven generations too – and sometimes a great deal more than that, on an ancient site with many layers of occupation and use.

> Tom still remembers all too well one horrific example
> e of what *not* to do in the ethics of fieldwork.
>
> He'd been invited – though 'nagged' might be more accurate – to join a group of Australian dowsers on a field-trip to a supposed 'sacred site' up in the high forests east of Melbourne. Within moments of arrival, they were all prancing around with their rods and pendulums – "look, we're raising pyramids of energy!", they proclaimed, with squeals of excitement.
>
> But it wasn't what would usually be called a sacred site. It was in fact an ancient Aboriginal burial ground – which had last been used as a mass grave after a massacre by Anglos barely a century earlier.
>
> No-one had bothered to check; or if they had, they hadn't bothered to think about the ethics – or even the legalities – of being there at all. They apparently believed that by dowsing there they were 'healing the earth'; but what they were actually doing was desecrating a grave – many graves – in perhaps the most insulting manner possible. About which the site was not happy – not happy *at all*. Yet so lost were they, in their self-centred delusions, that they didn't even *notice* – that was what was so hard to bear…
>
> In short: please, please, *think* before you dig…?

For a longer-term project, we'll also plan to go at all times of day and night, in all seasons, and in all weathers. And this perhaps especially applies to the times when we really don't feel like going out – because, after all, if we're aiming to build a relationship with a site, we can't expect much if we're only a 'fair-weather friend'…

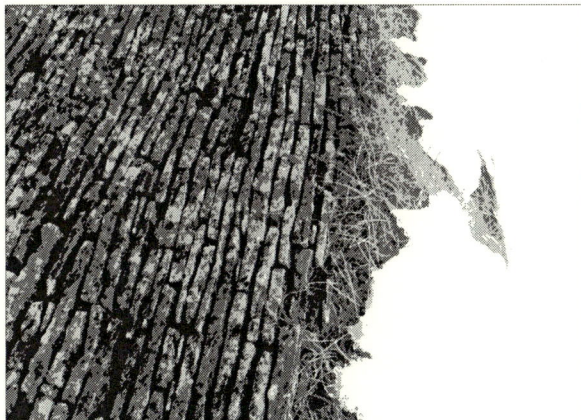
Wall of Belas Knap forecourt in snow

So we've done dowsing surveys and the like by torchlight, by candlelight, by starlight; we've done some of our work in pouring rain, in howling gales, in blizzards, in freezing fog, and sometimes even in good weather too. (Yes, even Britain has balmy days on rare occasion...) Which means we need to be prepared for almost anything – including wild changes in the mood-'weather' of the site itself. And time – and tim*ing* – will play an important part: sites often go through cyclic changes, such as solstice or Beltane, for example, and although many people would take the easier-seeming option of turning up on the nearest convenient weekend, we've often found there's been a real difference in 'feel' at the place if we do make the effort to be there on the actual night.

Another important part of preparation is somewhere to keep the results, both for future reference, and for planning-work.

For her archaeography work, Liz creates an Artist's equivalent of an 'incident room': one wall is covered with an ever-changing collage of drawings, photographs and diagrams, a whiteboard and plan-table stand ready for re-use, and easels hold the current works in progress.

Her current project aims to minimise disturbance to the site, so there are very few 'finds': on a side-table sit a Neolithic arrowhead turned up by the plough, a handful of flint-flakes from ancient axe-making, a few twigs, an unusual leaf, but that's about all. But for a more conventional archaeology survey, there would need to be a proper finds-table, a wet-room for cleaning and conservation, a fully-indexed catalogue and database, and somewhere to store it all.

Even for simple dowsing surveys, you'll still need some means to catalogue and store the results. If you plan for this *before* you start work, you'll have a better chance of finding it again afterwards!

And there's also preparation of ourselves – for example, for a dowsing session, assessing whether we can hold the disciplined focus that the Mystic mode requires during the dowsing work. If not, there's a choice: whether to change the plan for the session – for example, to shift more to the Artist, or the Scientist, as the primary mode – or to postpone the session until another day.

Once we've settled on that, it's time to move out.

Arriving on site

In our experience, the first five minutes on site are amongst the most crucial of the entire session.

First of all, we slow down from the journey – get out of 'driving mode', and spend a few minutes just sitting, doing nothing much. Put on the boots, perhaps, pull on jackets and anoraks, check the gear we'll be using. Slow down; *be* here now that we're here.

Next, another essential item: the 'Can I? May I? Am I ready?' checklist. We'll have done this already, as part of our planning and preparation before setting off; but we do it again here, before we start work. It's surprising how often things do change between departure and arrival... and if they do, we'll need to rethink our plan for the session. In particular, if there's anything more than a 'maybe' or a 'not quite yet' response to any questions, we may well need to pack up and go home: in this context as much as in others, 'No' *means* 'No' – and if we can't respect that, we shouldn't be attempting a relationship with the site at all...

There are also a few purely practical matters. If we're using a GPS, we'll need to switch it on straight away: it typically takes at least five minutes to find its full complement of satellite signals and settle down, and if we move off before it does so, it may well give us readings that are tens or even hundreds of metres off-track. And we also recheck vehicle security – windows, doors, nothing 'interesting' left visible in the back – and go through our checklists again: it's no fun having to run back and forth to the van when the work-site is half an hour's hike away across a ploughed field, or worse!

Then on to the site itself. In many cases we'll find there's a sort of 'watershed moment' – sometimes it's when the site first comes into view, at others at some kind of sensed boundary – when we seem to 'enter the presence' of the site. When that happens, we note the general 'feel', and again go through the 'Can I? May I? Am I ready?' checklist to ensure that we have an inner equivalent of the place's permission to continue.

> Even if we were to regard places as inanimate, it would probably still be wise to proceed as if they each had their own 'soul' – if only as a means to cope with the complexity of place.
>
> There's an Aboriginal tradition of announcing your own presence as you enter a site – who you are, where you come from, why you're there – and requesting its permission to be there. A kind of 'visitor visa', if you like; and also a way to engage the Mystic mode's need to establish a sense of 'belonging' to place.
>
> It seems a good idea to do this, even if only silently, when visiting any place – and also a good idea to respect any answer you might receive!

Once all of that has been completed successfully, it's time to unpack and get started on the session.

Fieldwork and records

Although there are two separate main themes here – the process of fieldwork, and the process of recording that fieldwork – we'll bundle them together in this section, because they'll usually take place at the same time.

Obviously, there are many, many ways in which fieldwork can be done. Here we've listed just three approaches that we use in our own work: dowsing, archaeography and GPS-mapped sensing.

Dowsing fieldwork

As we described earlier in *Dowsing in ten minutes* (p.7), there's really not that much to dowsing itself. We choose an instrument, choose something to work with, and go to it: that's about it, really. The rest depends on the work at hand, and perhaps even more on personal choice. For example, some of the ways you could specify what you're looking for would include:

- hold a sample of the target in your hand – a small bottle of water for water-divining, a Roman coin for Roman-period artefacts and so on
- hold a piece of paper with a text description of the target
- hold a photograph of a similar item, or a diagram that represents the target

- specify a 'signature' for the target – a pattern of instrument-responses, rather than a single response
- visualise the target, and hold that image in mind as you work
- describe the target under your breath as you work – "I'm looking for…"

You'll see there's a kind of gradation there from the physical to the virtual. The closer to the physical end of that spectrum you stay, the more reliable the dowsing is likely to be, so use physical samples and suchlike wherever you can. Of course, there's no possible physical sample for 'energy-lines' and the like, so there you'd have to use a virtual sample. But you still do have some choice: experiment to find what works best for you.

You should also have a repertoire of possible dowsing-responses, each with different meanings – see 'Know your instrument', back at p.8. And there'll be plenty of other suggestions in any of the good introductory books on dowsing – go look 'em up if you have any doubts. None of this is hard: it just takes practice – which is what fieldwork is all about.

The part that *is* hard – or hard*er*, fortunately – is in building and maintaining the disciplines. We need to choose one primary mode for the session – usually the Magician, for dowsing fieldwork – and use the other modes to support it. Once that's settled, we need to keep track both of the main discipline, and the tendency to wander off into the other disciplines – otherwise the quality of the work is put at risk. In effect, we need to know which mode to use at each moment, and which mode we're actually in at each moment – and take appropriate action if they're not the same!

> Again, this isn't as hard as it may sound. It's mostly just a matter of paying attention to what's going on, within you, and around you, whilst you're working.

In our experience, there's a useful analogy here between dowsing and massage-work – especially the way that intuition will cut in and out during a massage session – which illustrates well the interplay between the Magician, the Artist and the Mystic.

When we're doing massage-work with a client, for example, we would always start off with the techniques and sequences that we learned in formal training. That provides the 'ground' – a proven discipline of best-practice from the Magician, with focus held by that light-trance state of the Mystic – to which we know we can return to safely at any time.

102

When the Artist's intuition cuts in – and there's a definite difference in 'feel' when it does so – we switch over to follow whatever it indicates. We do so with care, though – we *don't* just abandon safety and follow it blindly. If it does seem to suggest something that would imply any pain or risk, we would usually bring it up with the client first, and note their response: often it'll point to an issue that *is* significant for the client, and will lead from there to some other approach that *does* work safely.

When the intuition drops out again – and again, there's a definite 'feel' to this, a kind of 'flatness', a clear sense of "I've lost it" that probably comes as much from the Mystic as from the Artist – we would first note that it *has* dropped out, and then return smoothly to the trained discipline.

> A quick warning here: trying to hold on to the intuition-mode when it's dropped out may not only be dangerous, but will all but guarantee its non-availability in the present and often in the future as well. *Not a good idea*…

In more general terms the trained discipline acts as both a safe default-pattern for activity – the Magician – and as a meditative focus – the Mystic – which allows intuition – the Artist – to cut in and out again as appropriate. The key point is that although the intuition-mode should, in principle, give better results for the *individual* needs in the context, it isn't stable enough, or reliable enough, to depend on throughout the session: the patterns learnt in training provide a fallback to ensure that *some* kind of discipline applies at all times.

So to translate this back to a dowsing context, we use the Magician and the Mystic to set up a standard search-pattern – "I am looking for water; the rods will cross over when they are directly above a water-line". Whilst doing that, we watch for any side-feelings that come from the Artist, note what they suggest, and if it seems appropriate, follow them for a while. As soon as the Artist drops out again, we return to the previous pattern – so again we maintain discipline throughout.

> The same applies when you don't seem to be getting any results at all, by the way. Don't be dejected about it, because that really *will* block the flow. Instead, just stick to the routine, so as to create space for the standard response to happen where appropriate, and also to allow any 'side-feelings' to pop up as and if they will.
>
> Remember that point about "in order to remember something you never knew, first set out to forget it": much the same often occurs in this type of context too. When nothing seems to be happening, what

often *is* happening in the background is a 'doing no-thing', a kind of hidden restructuring of the 'hologram'. If you leave enough space for that to happen, by allowing things to 'not-work' for a while, the result is often a sudden unexpected insight that seems to come 'out of the blue' a short while later.

When you see nothing happen, something *is* still happening – it's just that you probably won't know until later what it was that you saw. Panic not!

You'll notice there's been no mention of the Scientist so far – and that's with good reason, because during the dowsing work itself we actually need to keep the Scientist out of the picture as much as possible.

Remember the Plan/Do/Check/Act quality-cycle described in *The disciplined dowser* (see p.25). The Scientist has a role to play *before* the session, in using analysis to help us plan what we'll do in the session and how we're going to do it; and it has other roles *after* the session, to check and review what's been done, and help the Magician take action to improve the overall skill. But *during* a session the Scientist's only tasks are to keep track of location, and to do any record-keeping – and that's all.

The Scientist doesn't have any other active role during a session, because its neediness for certainty and repeatability will intrude too much in the flow of the work. We need each session, each movement, each setup and request for a dowsing response to be as if we've never done it before: otherwise the mind intrudes in the process, and we end up searching for whatever our expectations expect – which is not likely to give us the results we want…

In many ways, though, keeping track of location is probably one of the hardest parts of fieldwork. It's easy enough to set up the search, and – with a little practice – easy enough to get a response; but where *is* the response? How do we identify where that is? How do we mark it? That can be a lot trickier than it sounds – especially when working solo.

This particularly applies to marking the course of water-lines and other linear features. For a single-point response, it isn't too hard to drop a marker of some kind, or dig a small hole with the back of your heel; but for a linear feature you have to do this many times over – or, preferably, mark the feature with a continuous line.

Sounds simple enough, but often not so easy in practice. "You cannot use string if there are cattle in the field", warned the veteran dowser Guy Underwood back in the 1950s, "because they will eat it. It is disconcerting to both parties to have to pull many yards of string or tape measure from their cuds, and it spoils the tape measure..."

Scraped grass to mark edge of dowsed feature at Belas Knap

Some present-day dowsers use spray-cans for this, or tow a leaky bag of flour to mark a trail as they move along. In her dowsing work at Belas Knap and elsewhere, Liz tends to scrape out a line with mown grass, or snow, or any other material that happens to be to hand – or foot, in this case!

A GPS can also help in this, despite its relative lack of precision, because it can create a trail of 'trackpoints' automatically as you walk. You'll need to mark the start and end of each section of water-line or whatever with a manual 'waypoint' on the GPS; and you may also need to change the settings in the GPS itself to get it to record trackpoints at more frequent intervals than in its default configuration. Very useful as auto-documentation for a quick preliminary survey.

Working solo, you have to switch briefly into the Scientist mode to mark each location – and it's easy to lose the Mystic's focus when you do this. So there's no doubt that that part of the work *is* easier as a team: with two people, one can dowse whilst the other does all the Scientist work; and with three, one can place the markers whilst the third maintains the log-book, which means that the whole process moves along much faster.

A larger group of people, though, can easily get in each other's way. It's not so much of a problem when they're all looking for the same thing, working in parallel – one archaeologist said he was first convinced of the value of dowsing when he saw a line of dowsers come to halt exactly along the line of an Iron Age ditch of which there was no sign at all on the surface. But when they're all looking for different things, in different ways, and with different search-patterns, it's not just that they'll get entangled with each other in a physical sense, it seems to happen in an energetic sense too – all manner of strange interferences, all picking up responses from each other, and so on. So the general recommendation here is that unless you have good reason to do otherwise, do keep the team small.

On a practical note, remember that dowsing can be surprisingly tiring – at times like driving in fog, straining the senses to reach out for even the smallest hint of information. So don't overdo it: break the dowsing down into relatively small chunks of time, take proper snack-breaks between them, keep the fluids up, and so on.

> Another safety-reason to keep food on hand is that it can act as a metaphoric 'fire-blanket' for the more minor hazards of the Reality Risk (see p.82). This is especially important when doing 'energy-dowsing' and suchlike, because it's easy to reach out too far into the imaginary space, sending the metabolism into a spiral that can often be disturbing and sometimes even dangerous. We keep a stick of Kendal Mint Cake – the old hikers' standby – in our field-bag for this, but something that's solid and starchy is even better to quickly 'ground' someone back in the everyday world: Liz loves a lump of the local lardy-cake!

Then there's the matter of how to record the dowsing work. If our primary mode is the Artist or the Mystic – in other words, the session is mostly about connecting with the 'feel' of place, closer to archaeography than conventional field-dowsing – we may not need much in the way of formal records: the feeling *is* the record, so to speak. But in any other case, and especially if we're aiming to share the results with others, we're going to need some kind of structured record. More to the point, if we *don't* record the results in an appropriate way, we may as well not do the work at all: it really *is* that simple.

> For field-dowsers, the 'bible' here would be CA Fortlage's *Dowse, Survey and Record*, available from the British Society of Dowsers.
>
> It's a compact, spiral-bound book, designed for use in the field. And its sub-title is exactly correct: it's "an essential guide to simple surveying for dowsers". Quietly and competently, yet with a happily wry sense of humour, it covers pretty much everything you'd need for fieldwork surveys, and more besides – such as the surveyor's all-important signals for 'tea's up!' "Always find the oldest pensioner in the area who can probably describe the previous history of the site in great detail, if not with equally great accuracy", says Fortlage. "A few carefully distributed pints of beer can be very revealing"...
>
> There are sections on basic set-up and preparation; surveys with compass, with measuring-tape and level; 'booking' survey-points in a

log-book; building a plan; and practical problems such as surveying around walls or over rivers. Just about the only thing the book doesn't cover, in fact, is the use of a GPS as a survey-tool – and that's probably because in most cases GPS isn't accurate enough for proper surveys.

Very strongly recommended – and not just for dowsers!

Structured records are not hard: once again, it's just a matter of discipline, in this case making appropriate entries in a log-book. The process may seem tedious at first, but without it, the Scientist would have nothing on which to work – so in the long run it's definitely worthwhile.

Before you start work, create a header-record for the session that would typically include the following:

- *identifier* – anything that would uniquely identify the overall session
- *when* – date and time
- *where* – name or description of location, coordinate-system in use (longitude / latitude, Ordnance Survey grid or whatever), coordinates of reference baseline used at the location, and so on
- *why* – brief summary of the purpose of the session, and references to any other source-documents supporting that purpose
- *who* – list of people involved in the session, and their roles in the session
- *what* – list of equipment used
- *how* – dowsing-samples used, methods used

After that, create an entry in the log each time anything significant occurs. Each entry for the session should typically include some or all of the following:

- *identifier* – anything that would uniquely identify the entry, at least within the session
- *when* – timestamp for the entry
- *where* – coordinates relative to the reference-baseline – initially often the identifier for the marker, with coordinates derived by survey-work later
- *who* – the person or people doing the active role for the entry – for example the dowser rather than the person who placed the marker for the event
- *cue* – the dowsing-sample in use, for example

- *response* – how the rods responded at this location, a description of the 'side-feeling', or suchlike
- *interpretation* (if appropriate) – implied meaning of the response
- *references* – identifiers for any photographs, notes, drawings or other artefacts associated with the specific event

As usual, be a little bit cautious about the 'interpretation' part of any event-record. If what you're doing is a straightforward search for underground pipes using a physical sample, and you get a straightforward 'X marks the spot' response, you can be fairly certain about the interpretation. But if you're doing any kind of non-physical work, or you get an unexpected or unusual response – just one rod coming across, for example, or both rods swinging outward – then it's best to flag as tentative any interpretation you make. Or use a Fortean approach, and skip the interpretation entirely.

> As mentioned earlier, one practical complication here is that if you're working solo, you'll need to switch into the Scientist mode to record the entry, and switch back again when you've finished. It's a lot easier if someone else is doing the note-taking for you...
>
> If you *are* working solo, you may find a GPS unit useful, despite its relative lack of accuracy, because it automatically records the identifier, the timestamp and a reasonable approximation of the location. If you then use the same identifier in the log-book, that's half of the work done for you at the push of a button. Handy.

At the end of the session, also add reference to other artefacts such as any notes, photographs, drawings and tests created during the session which aren't already linked to a single entry. If you do an after-action review for the session, as described later on p.117, attach that record here as well.

In addition to the main 'event-records', though, it's important to keep an eye – and all the other senses – open for other information that may wander in from a variety of unexpected directions. Liz calls this "that open mind thing, really": the main focus is on whichever mode we've chosen as the primary for the session, but we also remember to allow each of the other modes their own space too. Some useful questions to ask here might include:

- What other response does my instrument want to show me? – what do I feel, or what images comes to mind, as it shows me that response?

- What is the Mask of this place? – in what medium and manner should that felt interaction (see p.84) be expressed?
- What do I sense in this place? – for examples of types of sensings you might come across, see the list later in the 'Sensing with GPS' subsection, on p.113.

All of this applies especially to the Artist, of course, because it's in that mode that most of these 'side-feelings' start to come through. Which is where the discipline of archaeography comes into the picture, because from a dowsing perspective, archaeography is almost all about working with those 'side-feelings' – and linking the two forms of fieldwork together is starting to produce some very interesting results.

Archaeography fieldwork

Like archaeoastronomy or archaeoacoustics, archaeography is still a relatively new sub-discipline within academic archaeology. (It's also described as 'deep mapping', though there are subtle differences between the two approaches – see the links in the Resources appendix on p.139.) It's a kind of intentional bridge between archaeology and art – across what would usually be diametrically-opposed modes of the Scientist and the Artist – leveraging the disciplines of each to connect the past to the present.

> Two of the best references here are art-historian Lucy Lippard's *Overlay*, from the art side, and *Figuring It Out*, by the respected archaeologist Colin Renfrew, from a more conventional archaeology perspective.
>
> For the link between people and place, and felt sense of 'local distinctiveness', one of the best sources is Common Ground's 'Parish Maps' project, documented in their book *From Place to PLACE*.
>
> Take a look, too, at Liz's website for her archaeography work around the Belas Knap long-barrow, at bk.lizpw.com.

Although it often doesn't use dowsing *per se*, archaeography does share many of the same characteristics: most is focussed on sensings in an identified location, with the aim of deriving some kind of meaning – though here the boundary between personal and collective, subjective and objective, is often intentionally blurred.

Preparation for archaeography will usually involve an intense immersion in the formal archaeology of the site. In Liz's work at Belas Knap, this included photography of skulls and other artefacts from various 'digs' there; poring over air-photos and excavation-reports both for the site itself and nearby sites from the

Neolithic period to Roman and later; and reviewing folklore and legend from the entire surrounding region. The archaeology-oriented side of the fieldwork may include anything from a field-walk to search for artefacts turned up by the plough, to working with a research-crew using an experimental geophysics-scan system, to assessing rock-art and graffiti that span several millennia right up to the present day. Oh, and dowsing too, of course.

Tree in woods below Belas Knap

Then there's the more art-oriented side to the fieldwork. For example, this might well include photographing some part of the site in any of its infinitely different moods, or sketching inside the stone chambers or out amongst the nearby trees. There may be a cross-over to archaeoacoustics, testing and recording the sounds made by tapping on different stones. Some might simply be to set up conversations with holidaying tourists, or hikers on the long-distance footpath that crosses the site, to gain a sense of people's personal response to place. Other explorations with an artist's eye help to place the site within its surrounding landscape, breaking free of the artificial boundary between 'sacred' and 'profane' – and, perhaps more important from an archaeology perspective, the equally-artificial, all-too-literal boundary between protected and unprotected in a heritage-regulations sense.

110

Belas Knap from north field, with sheep

At times, too, this may well cross back over to the mainstream archaeology in other ways. At Belas Knap, the dowsing and the archaeography alike both seem to point out the site of another possible previously-unrecorded round-barrow close to the existing long-barrow, and possible extensions of the 'forecourt' into the as-yet-unexplored field in front. In such contexts the loose Artist mode needs to be balanced with the precision of the Scientist, mapping feelings and responses accurately in the sitescape and landscape so as to be usable to other researchers.

False-portal lintel and wall, Belas Knap

The records of the fieldwork necessarily reflect the same wide-open range: anything from artwork to physical artefacts, from broad brush-strokes to fully-dimensioned maps and charts. But – and we perhaps need to re-emphasise this point – each record needs to match the respective primary mode of Artist or Scientist or whatever. Maps and diagrams may have their own aesthetic, perhaps, but personal ideas and images and impressions should *never* be presented as 'fact'.

Sensing with GPS

For some while now we've been experimenting with a somewhat extreme merging of the Artist and Scientist modes in archaeography, building maps of sensings and other observations in a systematic way with a GPS unit. This seems to be a new technique, so we'll describe it in some detail.

> There are some possible cross-links with another formal discipline called 'psychogeography' – popularised by Will Self's column of the same name in the London newspaper *The Independent* – because some of its practitioners do use GPS units to map felt responses to place. The difference is that there it's mainly used in cities, and with a more present-day political bent – at the level of the everyday 'litany of complaint' rather than deep-myth, to use the terms from Causal Layered Analysis. To our knowledge, this is the first time this GPS-based technique has been used in archaeography or any related discipline.

The basic principle is straightforward enough: just walk around with a notebook and a GPS, and record whatever happens to be noticed. The GPS handles the Scientist mode's need for precise location, freeing the Artist mode to concentrate on the separate precision of the sensings It's not *quite* as simple as that in practice, of course – but not that much more so.

One practical concern is the type of GPS unit to use. The common 'sat-nav' type won't do the job well: you *can* use them for a first experiment or two, but they're optimised to work with roadmaps, and tend to get confused off-road, hunting for roads that don't exist. Instead, it's better to use a GPS unit that's made for hikers, and preferably one with a 'high-precision' sensor that can locate to within ten feet or less. These will automatically record a trail of movement from switch-on to switch-off, usually auto-generating new 'trackpoint' markers several times a minute; and they also allow the user to set manual 'waypoints' – the latter being what we use to tag the selected sensings.

For the record, the GPS unit we use at present is a Garmin eTrex Legend HC – a hiker's model at the lower-end of the price-range. It's supplied with its own Garmin MapSource software, but we also use another mapping program, GPS Utility, which can create layered maps with links to other references such as Google Earth – you'll find more details and a free-trial version at www.gpsu.co.uk.

So the process we use is as follows:

- pre-select a route to follow – perhaps around the perimeter of the site, or a predefined search-pattern generated by the GPS itself or by an external program
- each time there's a clear sensing of some kind, or the route crosses some relevant feature – especially a fixed marker such as a survey-baseline or a field-corner – set a waypoint on the GPS, and record the observation in the log-book together with the GPS-generated waypoint reference-number
- at the end of the session, save the GPS's automatically-generated trail and waypoint-log into the respective computer program
- update the waypoint-log to include the observations from the handwritten log, to link the observations to their respective locations – and then store this as a permanent record of the session
- use the software to create a map that includes the track and the marker-tags for each waypoint
- optionally, cross-reference this map to previous sessions, or to official maps, site-plans, air-photographs and other sources of verified locations and other relevant information

In accordance with the Artist mode's principle of 'anything goes', the sensings can be anything at all – whatever we happen to notice that seems somehow relevant. When working as a pair, usually what we look for are body-sensations that we both notice at the same time – though the sensations themselves may not be the same for each of us. To give a few examples, these might include:

- sudden headache or other pain that seems linked to place
- a sense of a sudden energy, often felt along the spine
- a sense of being pulled in some direction – up, down, sideways, round
- sensations of 'required' movement – marching, or arm-movements or the like

- a scent, taste or general 'feel' – particularly a sort of 'taste of tin' that seems to be characteristic of a specific energy in a place
- sights or sounds that seem to want to be noticed, so to speak – sudden flight of birds, butterflies, a fold in the landscape, or a sudden sense of deep quiet
- any particular feelings from the place, such as "we should not be here – not a good place to be", "a women's space", "a quiet space, a healing space" and so on – though note that these are recorded in a Fortean sense, *without* theory or interpretation
- any changes noted in the overall context, such as tiredness from prevailing wind, climbing, uneven ground and so on, which might be relevant for adjusting future interpretation

> Liz also has a particular interest in animal-tracks and foraging-places – especially the persistent trails of large animals such as badgers or deer – because these represent *non*-human long-term interactions with a 'human' place. So we'll usually record the locations of these as well, though they may not be so relevant for other archaeographers. Think of those points as an interesting type of optional extra, if you like.

One other practical issue to note is that it's important to hold the GPS steady and level, pointing in the forward direction as much as possible. Impressive though it is, GPS technology is still fairly rudimentary, and its precision is easily upset by careless handling: waving the GPS unit around whilst walking can increase any inaccuracies many times over. One of the reasons we prefer to work as a pair in GPS-sensing is that doing so helps to protect accuracy, because one person uses the GPS whilst the other writes the notes. Working on one's own, it's hard to keep the GPS steady when switching back and forth to write notes in the log-book.

> Another reason for being fussy about this point is that we've quite often noted what we might call 'GPS anomalies' – places where the recorded track seems to go off course for no apparent reason, by distances which are significantly more than the normal tolerances. Following along a fence-line, for example, the recorded track will usually wander from side to side by no more than a couple of feet at most; but then will suddenly assert that we've somehow jumped sideways by twenty feet or more – though in reality we've kept going in the same straight-line path.
>
> There may be a simple physical or technical explanation, of course – a change in the available set of satellite-signals, perhaps. Yet in most cases where these anomalies have occurred, we've also recorded specific sensings – though we won't know this until we get to compare the log-book and the track-record some time later, after the session.

There'll need to be a lot more study before anything certain can be confirmed, so for now we're sticking to a strict Fortean approach – no theory, no interpretation. But interesting, nonetheless…

Overall, there are quite a few advantages to this technique. It's a little more sophisticated than dowsing with coat-hanger rods, but the equipment is still relatively simple: the only significant item is the GPS itself, and they're getting cheaper and more capable every year. Linked to suitable software – often bundled with the unit itself, or available free elsewhere – the GPS track and waypoints are aligned automatically with the coordinate-grids on Ordnance Survey maps and the like; some programs can also merge multiple overlays from, say, a base-map, an air-photograph and several sensing-sessions, all into a single composite image. And the technique can be used almost anywhere: in long grass, over rough scrub or in treed areas, and in many other contexts where conventional survey-techniques would be difficult at best. There's a lot of versatility there.

As for disadvantages, it's true it does demand a lot of experience with subjective self-observation – quite a bit more than for routine dowsing. But the main problem is lack of precision for locations: although some specialist GPS equipment can pin a location down to within an inch or less, the types of units that most people could afford are only certain to within ten feet at best. That's at least ten times less precise than a skilled dowser – a *big* difference if someone were to plan an excavation on the basis of those results!

In any case, it's early days with the technique, and correlations with other survey-techniques are still some way off. To be honest, we still don't have much of an idea as yet about what any of it means, or how to *use* it – let alone expect to be able to pinpoint, say, the precise edge of a Neolithic ditch and embankment, something that an experienced archaeological dowser could do with relative ease. But there's a definite sense that *something* worthwhile is going on: so a case of Watch This Space, perhaps?

Closing the session

At the end of a session, it's essential to ensure that it really *is* the end of the session.

This isn't a simple truism: the point here is to mark an explicit boundary between one way of working and the next. For dowsers especially, this can be a literal matter of life and death: driving whilst still in 'dowsing mode' is a serious safety hazard, because a steering-wheel happens also to have all of the characteristics of a good dowsing instrument... don't dowse and drive!

For strictly-physical fieldwork this may perhaps be less critical, though it seems likely it's always a good idea in any case. But if the work involved any type of 'imaginary energies' – such as in most dowsing surveys, and particularly in sensing for 'entities' and the like – it's crucial to create closure, because of real concerns from the Reality Risk (see p.82).

A traditional magician would talk about 'closing the circle' here, whilst aircraft pilots might summarise their post-landing check-lists, but it's much the same process whichever way we describe it: we need some kind of routine ritual – whether formal or casual – to mark that boundary. Like the pilot, a checklist can be useful here – if only to ensure that all the gear is correctly stowed, and nothing has been left behind on the field.

Perhaps the simplest example, though, would be to *stop*: take a deliberate, intentional break of a few minutes to slow down and disconnect from the site. Breathe. Relax. The work is done; it's over.

> Another variant would be simply to say 'Thank you' to the site!
>
> Politeness apart, this kind of personification of relationship with place is common to many traditional cultures, as we saw earlier with the Aboriginal notion of requesting a 'visitor visa' to the place. In that sense, saying 'Thank you' closes the space that we opened with the 'Can I? May I? Am I ready?' checklist.
>
> From the perspective of the Magician mode, it's also known to work well, as a means to create closure – and in practice, that's what matters most!

There's also what we might describe as physiological safety. Most fieldwork can be surprisingly tiring: you're likely to need to bring your energy back up before you drive off. (This in itself can form a useful ritual boundary – "I had a cup of tea!", says Liz.) But remember too that many types of intuitive work – of which dows-ing is just one example – require us to be in a state of light trance in order to do the work: as mentioned earlier, food and drink can also be important as a means to come down out of that state, and return safely to the 'normal' world. So it's not just energy that's needed here, but something 'grounding', something starchy and solid – a sandwich or a cereal-bar, a doughnut or a danish-pastry.

If you've been doing a lot of dowsing-work in a single session out in the field, don't skip this step: it could literally save your life.

On a less serious note, what could also save your work, and improve quality overall, is an 'after action review'. As the name suggests, it's something that should be done straight away as soon as the work is complete. It consists of just four questions:

- What was supposed to happen?
- What actually happened?
- What caused the difference?
- What could we learn from this, or what could we do differently next time, to improve the results?

> If you're working with a team, there's also just one additional rule for an after-action review, called, "pin your stripes at the door" – you each had your own roles and responsibilities in the team, so no-one's opinion is necessarily any 'better' than another's here.

The usual suggestion is to spend a quarter of the time on the first two questions, a quarter of the time on the third, and fully half of the time on the last. The answers can sometimes be surprising – and often embarrassing, unfortunately – but always worthwhile: it's how we learn anew, and improve our skills.

> Sometimes there may not seem to have been any result at all. If so, don't be downhearted about this: don't forget that, to the Scientist, a negative result is just as significant as a positive one.
>
> Some years back, Liz spent many months going over and over a field next to the main Crickley Hill habitation site near Cheltenham, convinced that there had to be some strong connection between them. She tried everything she knew: dowsing, fieldwalking, plant analysis and the rest. But at the end of all that work, her only result was a single flint arrowhead, which she'd found right on the field boundary with the main site. Nothing else; *nothing*.
>
> Yet that 'nothing' was still an important outcome. As a result of all that work – yet also only because of the care and precision in that work – we now know that there's nothing in that field. That fact is significant in itself.
>
> To an archaeologist, of course, the next question would be to ask *why* there's nothing there, when it's so close to a major habitation used by several different cultures over several thousand years. But that's a question that comes *after* the fieldwork, and need not concern us here!

Whatever you do, don't be despondent about it: getting anywhere meaningful with dowsing and the like takes time, and practice, practice, practice. But it's not a *lot* of time: as a comparison, it's generally reckoned that it takes about a hundred hours of regular practice to start getting somewhere worthwhile with playing a flute, and dowsing is probably not that much different. A hundred hours is only two hours a week for a year: it's not much. Truly.

Let's be blunt about this: you're not going to learn much of anything useful solely from a book, or from a single New Age-style weekend workshop. What you learn there will only start to make sense when it's put into practice out in the field, week after week. Most people overestimate what can be done in a single weekend, but equally *under*estimate what they can do in a year; imagine, then, what you could do in a decade of consistent, careful fieldwork. A *lot*, is the short answer. So go to it, perhaps?

In any case, do get out there – get out of the armchair, and out into the field! Engage all of the modes – Artist, Scientist, Mystic, Magician – in all aspects of that work; and have fun whilst you're doing it – of course!

PRACTICE – WORKED EXAMPLES

Techniques summary

Dowsing and geomancy – For dowsing, we both use angle-rods as the main instrument for fieldwork. (Tom's are mild-steel, Liz's are brass, in case such things may matter for future researchers!) If the weather is too rough for angle-rods, Tom will also use a heavy brass plumb-bob as a pendulum – somewhat less versatile than the rods, but less affected by strong winds. The main emphasis in dowsing is water-lines and other underground features, though Tom also does some assessments for perceived above-ground 'energies'. In the past, we've both usually recorded our dowsing surveys in a somewhat ad-hoc manner, using any available materials as markers, and photographing the results; more recently, we've aimed to follow the guidelines in CA Fortlage's *Dowse, Survey and Record* (see p.106) – though we wouldn't claim that fabled level of precision as yet! As will be seen from the examples, Liz also identifies and records other types of geomantic impressions, usually in the form of drawings or diagrams.

Sensing with GPS - For this work we use the GPS-sensing technique described in the 'Fieldwork and records' section (see p.112). Sensings are recorded on the spot with a notebook, with entries linked to the waypoint-ID generated by the GPS. At the end of the session, the tracks and trackpoints are downloaded to mapping-software; we then merge the sensing-records from the notebook into the resultant data-set. The final record is a single document-file containing the map of the track and waypoints, the merged data-set of waypoints and sensings, the full list of recorded track-points, and copies of any photographs or other artefacts gathered during the session.

Photography and illustration – Most of the photography for the work we've described here has been in digital format, using a variety of cameras with image-sizes in the four to eight-megapixel range. Liz also uses film-cameras, including a Pentax SLR and a pinhole-camera – in part for the broader artistic possibilities, but

119

also because it seems that some events and effects can be recorded only on film. Some digital imagery has also been post-processed in Photoshop or PaintShop Pro, or used as baselines for digital drawings in ArtRage. Liz will often create drawings, illustrations and diagrams on-site, mainly in pen, pencil or charcoal, though in other media as well; Tom also attempts occasional scratchy sketches, usually with a brush-pen, though also with a graphite-stick or conté-crayon.

Belas Knap, Winchcombe, near Cheltenham

Belas Knap has been Liz's main focus of interest for some years, with work covering the full scope of archaeography, from field-walking, rock-art analysis and geophysics at the archaeology end of the scale, through to dowsing and other location-mapped sensing, and photography, painting, drawing, sculpture and performance at the art end. For here, we'll emphasise examples from the intuitive-skills domains, but in practice the archaeography is – and needs to be – a seamless whole, integrating information from the entire scope.

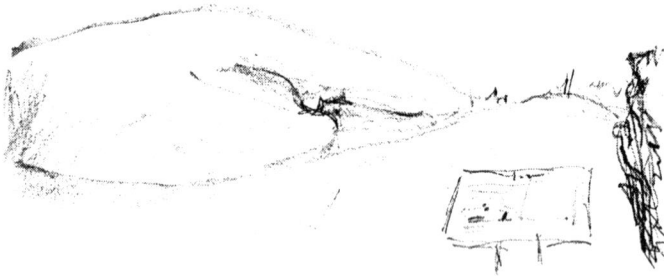

Belas Knap – forecourt from entrance-gate at north-east

The main part – or rather, the best-known part – of the site is the Belas Knap long-barrow, dating from the Neolithic period. It's sited at the top of a steep wooded ridge, at SP 021 254 on the British National Grid reference. Its structure is what's known as a 'Severn-Cotswold' type, with a false-entrance between the two horns of the north-facing forecourt, and four small stone chambers cut into the mound, one on the west side, two on the east, and one (now reconstructed as an open cist) at the south end. The mound itself is about 160 feet (50m) long, 60 feet (18m) wide at the forecourt end, and almost fifteen feet (4m) high at its highest point,

120

just south of the false-portal. It's been much-excavated and much-'restored' over the past couple of centuries, but is believed to be fairly close now to the original layout for the later period – though the side-chambers are likely to have had corbelled 'beehive' ceilings rather than their present flat-roofed reconstructions.

Yet as with so many other ancient sites, the barrow is only a centrepiece within a much larger landscape. Air-photographs and other archaeological evidence indicate that there's a round-barrow from a later period in the adjoining field to the west; Liz's work suggests there could be another, and maybe more, slightly further to the south. Liz has found flakes of flint from Neolithic tool-making out at the far end of that field, some six hundred yards (500m) or more to the west, which also suggests intensive activity over a broader area than just the barrow itself. Then there's the steep slope of woodland below the barrow, and the dome of the ridge in the next field to the north – all of which may well hold key information about the broader site.

Multiple sessions, barrow area, January-July 2008

The image below is a copy of a small six-by-four card (15cm x 10cm) which Liz keeps in her car, and has reworked in the Artist mode after each visit to the Belas Knap site.

Belas Knap, composite drawing – Artist mode

East is at the top of the drawing; the long-barrow is shown in the upper-centre, with the horns of the forecourt at its northern end of the barrow facing left. Each line represents something that Liz has sensed in the landscape. Working in this way over an extended period of time builds a depth and richness to the picture that is not available from the results of a single session.

Many of the same energetics-features and tracks immediately to the west and south (below and to the right) of the barrow can also be seen in the next image. Some lines and features also extend into the field to the north (left) and into the woodland sloping steeply down the ridge to the east (above).

Multiple sessions, barrow and west field, April-June 2008

This figure is a composite, showing the results of several sessions by Liz, to build up an overview of the northern part of the west field prior to scheduled ploughing. The long-barrow, on the eastern side of the field, is shown here at the top, as an elongated oval, with the northern forecourt to the left.

In effect, this is an Artist-mode representation of dowsing in the Magician mode, study of animal-tracks and other features in the Scientist mode, and subjective self-observation of response to place in the Artist and Mystic modes. There's a descriptive key at the bottom-right of the graphic, which summarises the different types of marks and their respective meanings.

Water-lines and other dowsing responses appear as lines that wind and loop from side to side. The straighter lines represent animal-tracks, usually made by made by badgers or deer – the small ovals mark the positions of junctions or passing-points, as recorded in Liz's photos of the tracks. The triangles represent areas where there were strong shifts in overall feeling, with the larger dark ovals indicating clearly-bounded places where the feel was particularly 'heavy' and depressing. The larger circle somewhat below (or west) of the long-barrow may correspond with the archaeologists' suspected round-barrow; at the least, it does seem to match a similar feature that's evident in the set of 1950s aerial-archaeology photographs that Liz obtained soon after this work was complete.

Because this work was done primarily in the Artist mode, the location of each feature shown will only be approximate, though the relative positions of the features should be correct.

Belas Knap west field (barrow to top) – emphasis on Artist mode

Sensing session, long-barrow, June 2008

This diagram by Liz describes the results of a sensing session at Belas Knap, showing the kind of symbolic imagery that is typical of the Mystic mode – rather than expressive, as in the Artist mode, or illustrative, from the Scientist or Magician.

The session covered just the mound itself, from the bank just to the north of the forecourt – here shown at the top of the drawing – to the small cist at the south.

Each symbol or icon describes the feel or movement of energy experienced at various points around the mound.

First there is a back-and-forth swirl along the bank that encloses the forecourt. There are what feel like waves within the forecourt itself, and a sense of upward-moving energy beside and within the drystone walls either side of the false-portal. The portal itself seems solid, unmoving, dark. On the banks above the drystone walls, angling upward to the slight peak of the mound, the energy seems to move southward on the west side, and northward on the east.

There is a kind of 'spine' along the centre-line of the barrow, clearly visible in its physical shape – though most probably worn by visitors' feet – which also appears here as an energetic axis for the mound. Between the portal and the two northerly side-chambers, there is a strong sense of a diagonal flow of energy across the spine. The perceived movement of energy within each of the two side-chambers is somewhat similar, a feeling of bars or waves of energy, yet that on the east side is sensed as a kind of rotation contained entirely within the chamber, whilst that on the west is experienced as having a twisting motion, pushing waves of energy outward through the mouth of the chamber.

The low south-east chamber has a very different feel: the energy here seems to scintillate, appearing and disappearing like motes of dust in sunlight, yet without any clear sense of movement even within the confines of the chamber.

Finally, over and round the remains of the southernmost chamber, in line with the axis of the barrow, the energy is experienced as moving in a diagonal direction, much as at the peak behind the false-portal. The difference here is that the energy seems to flow in both directions, north-west to south-east and south-east to north-west, rather than only the latter, as at the peak.

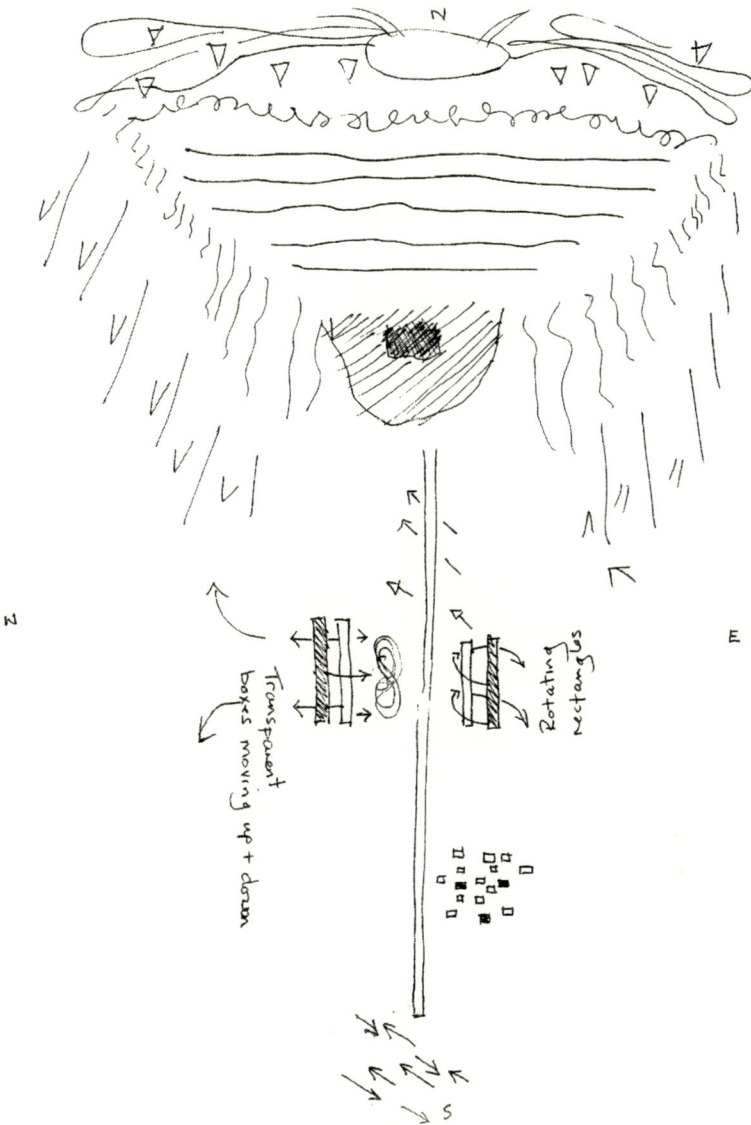

Belas Knap barrow (north at top) – emphasis on Mystic mode

It's important, though, to remember that all of this is subjective experience, not 'fact'. In this case it does tally well with the some-what more concrete results of dowsing for water-lines, but even that, of course, would not be considered to be fact in a scientific sense unless we were to dig down and find the water – which we wouldn't be allowed to do on a listed heritage-site such as Belas Knap! Yet whilst we insist that subjective sensing in the Artist or Mystic modes should never be taken as fact in itself, it *can* provide useful pointers to possible fact that could be assessed in later sessions in the Scientist or Magician modes. That *is* the way we use this kind of work; though also as input to, and as, an archaeographic art-form in its own right, of course.

Preparation for sessions in north field, July 2008

This field is immediately to the north of the listed heritage-area around the Belas Knap barrow.

Some instant Artist-mode impressions: It's just a field. It's quite big. It has sheep in it. It's sort of domed in shape. It has a footpath running through it. And that's about it, really. Now what do we do?

Call in the Scientist-mode first. A quick check on the Ordnance Survey map shows it's a sort of stretched rectangle, tilted a bit to the north-west, at about SP 019 258 at the top right and SP 018 254 at bottom-left, somewhere around nine hectares or 22 acres in area. The map also shows that the boundary between the old parishes of Winchcombe and Charlton Abbots runs along the southern edge of the field: interesting, but may not be relevant.

A bit more detail about that footpath. It's part of the Cotswold Way long-distance path, though that's a modern 'walker's trail' rather than a centuries-old trading-track. This segment connects the long-barrow to the car-park a kilometre or so away on the road to the north-east. The footpath runs through the trees along the eastern edge of the field.

Search the literature and the Net for more about its archaeology and land-use. No record of ploughing in recent times, which means any archaeological structures below the surface are likely to be reasonably intact – that's good news, anyway. Air-photos: a few available, including some taken specifically for archaeology, but nothing visible in any of those. Check the archaeology record: discover there isn't any for here – hmmm… Plenty of other sites nearby, though, including a whole swag of Roman villas along the valley below. And information about a peculiar ancient 'cuculati' cult in the general region, with strange hooded figures popping up in the archaeology and in various folklore forms over a couple of millennia at least – might be relevant from an archaeography perspective too.

Next, call in the Magician mode to start working on a plan. First option would be: a mixture of archaeography and dowsing. But what kind of archaeography? What kind of dowsing? How would we link this to the main Belas Knap site? The Magician will need to mediate a conversation with both the Scientist and the Artist to derive some suitable ideas for this. Some outcomes of that conversation:

- look for 'local distinctiveness' – grasses, stony patches, insects, evidence of animal and bird activity; also any unusual sound or scent
- engage the 'fieldwalking mind' – watch for flints, hummocks, dry patches that might indicate something just under the surface
- explore boundary-effects and 'liminal space', both physical and felt – the present-day wall *separates* the field from the local 'focus-place'; likewise the internal boundary between private and public represented by the footpath
- we *presume* there's a connection with Belas Knap – the 'forecourt' of Belas Knap faces into this field, and is barely five metres beyond the modern wall, so it seems likely that at the least there would be some 'overspill' – but we need to *test* that assumption!

The footpath is interesting, from a feelings perspective, because there's an interesting inversion: the 'private space' of the field is open, exposed, whereas the 'public space' of the footpath is enclosed, like a tunnel under the trees.

We want to do more than just a quick scan here, so we'll need permission from the landowner, and maybe other stakeholders, too, to do more detailed exploration. With luck that shouldn't be too hard, because we're not aiming to do any digging or destructive testing, and it looks like it's outside of the Heritage remit.

All of this sets the context for the project, anyway.

Mixed-mode session, north field, July 2008

For this work-session, we start with archaeography.

The way of approach seems important. We've come via the west route to Belas Knap, so we see the field first from between the two horns of the forecourt. The dome-shape of the field is very noticeable from here, rising gently upward from the forecourt, along the line of the ridge. But most people now would see it a very different way: there's the long slog up from the car-park, then a brief breathing-space in the open before entering the tunnel-like path under the trees, with Belas Knap itself appearing, almost unexpected, as the path opens out at the end of the tunnel.

There's a real danger, too, of equating the ancient landscape with that of the present – now woodland all the way up the steep slope of the ridge, then open meadow at the top. Liz recalls the archaeological evidence on this: "The whole area seems to have been much more heavily wooded than at present; the current thought is that the mound was in a small clearing in the wood, with cut sight-lines and processional ways." When we look at the context, though, this doesn't seem to make sense. The mound is right on the edge of the ridge, but isn't actually at the highest point – that's in the field we're about to explore. Given the evidence elsewhere of the importance of intervisibility over long distances, what's going on here, if the site's on a ridge that's mostly woodland? And where *are* those supposed 'processional ways'?

Everywhere we look, we keep seeing the need for the help of specific specialists to populate our 'hologram': forest-change; land-clearance; water-usage and water-management; geophysics; geology; field-search; botany; wildlife, even *snails*, for heaven's sake. And we're going to need to collect stories of the present as well as of the past – which means a lot of conversations with 'ordinary people', non-specialists such as the tourists who come visiting the site. Even a project as small as this one starts to feel unmanageable once we realise we need to include *everything*…

A brief rest, then change over to do GPS-sensing.

We set out to do a counter-clockwise circuit of the field, starting at the gate at the former end of the footpath, in the south-east corner. (A few years back, the path was moved a few metres to the west, with a new swing-gate in the stone wall – part of the Cotswold Way upgrade, apparently.) This takes almost an hour, picking out various useful reference-points – pylons, field-edges, gates, a marker for a long-distance gas-pipe – but no sensing-impressions till we get to the south edge of the field, just under two hundred metres west of the long-barrow. After that, the sensings continue all the way past the mound: one example is "want to turn left – being pushed left in an arc; smell of burning tin"; another, just to the west of the mound, is "feeling light-headed, disoriented – want to lie down".

> Once again, we're careful not to put any interpretation on those sensings – after all, some may be just straightforward side-effects of our walking up and down a steep hill for an hour or more. We simply log each sensing, together with its location, and move on.
>
> Any process of Scientist-mode interpretation would happen much later, and only when there are sufficient data from multiple sessions – or correlations with other areas of interest – to make further analysis and interpretation worthwhile.

After that, we change over to dowsing.

Which is not a good move, given that we've already been at it for some hours, and we've been hit by instant exhaustion from that last section of the circuit.

No clear plan of what to do: we just go straight to it, vaguely wandering around in the area on the slope twenty to fifty metres to the north of the forecourt. Tom uses heavy-weight angle-rods, with a mental search-pattern of "anything tangible of significant archaeological interest", walking in a grid-pattern with about five-metre spacings; the result is various uninterpretable pointers toward the wooded area to the east. Liz uses lighter-weight rods, looking for "archaeological edges", for which the result is a set of marker flags that 'ramble round the shire', giving no clear sense of any kind of edge at all.

We don't record any of it – not even photographs. So in some ways a good example of what *not* to do for a dowsing-session…

But overall, the session does provide some context and useful 'first impressions', and suggests that, yes, it's worth doing further exploration.

And later, as we start to drive away, a chance meeting with the landowner, walking her dogs – from which we gain formal per-mission for further work. Which is good, and much-appreciated.

Dowsing at barrow and in north field, September 2008

This session was a follow-up to previous work here by Liz, dowsing for water-lines in the forecourt and along the length of the mound. The aim was for Tom to do an independent check of the nominal lines that Liz had found, and if the two sets of results *did* tally, to follow the lines further into the north field.

A first requirement here is to lock out the Scientist mode from the dowsing as much as practicable, because if we're doing an independent check, the one thing we *don't* want is influence from any previous results – tests for repeatability come *after* the session, not during it! So there's detailed discussion about where to look, and what to look for, but also a careful avoidance of even any hints about what to expect.

Given the context, Tom will do the dowsing for this section, with Liz placing flags at each key-point or change of direction, and keeping track of any notes – though we're hindered somewhat by the fading light of oncoming dusk, and by intermittent heavy rain, which makes notetaking a damp and rather difficult exercise...

Tom switches into the Mystic mode, for focus in dowsing, backed up by the Artist for sensing, whilst Liz switches to the Scientist mode for her tasks here. The overall mode for both is the Magician, since we have a sizeable task to do in a limited amount of time.

Starting west-to-east across the forecourt, there's an immediate challenge to the Mystic to hold focus, because there's a great deal of interference – metaphorically speaking – from what feels like a very strong line of energy a metre or so above ground apparently moving northward from the false-portal. For this context, this isn't what we're looking for, but it does take some concentration and effort to block it out, and return the focus to searching for below-ground water.

Belas Knap – flags mark waterlines through the forecourt

The results suggest three clear water-lines moving out through the forecourt, all flowing northward: one starts at the eastern pillar of the portal, and veers quite strongly to the east as it clears the horn of the forecourt wall; one comes out of the western side of the same pillar, and moves in the general direction of straight outward from the portal; and the third comes out on the westward side of the other pillar, and moves somewhat westward as it clears the forecourt. There are a few less-strong lines – one follows along beside the east wall of the forecourt, becoming a bit confused in places with the other stronger eastern line; one flows *inward* at the tip of the western horn, whilst a counterpart seems to flow out from the eastern tip – but these seem to be the main ones here.

This is almost the exact same result as in Liz's previous sessions: the only real difference is that Liz had recorded a much stronger zigzagging of the lines. The lines do seem to be quite wide, though – perhaps as much as five or six feet (2m) – so there's a credible suggestion that Liz had 'bounced from side to side' of each line, so to speak, whilst Tom had focussed only on the effective centre.

Unfortunately, there's insufficient time to do a full measured survey, but the relative positions of the flags and respective lines are photographed and logged as the records for the session.

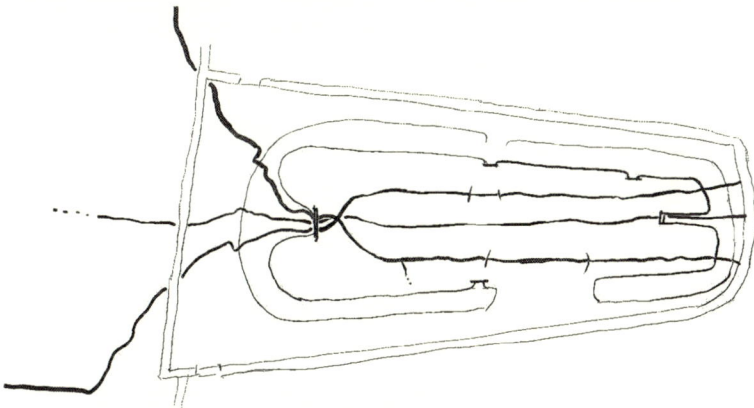

Belas Knap – sketch of waterlines along and beyond mound

The next stage is to follow the three main lines outward into the north field. This is new work, so both Tom and Liz take turns to dowse, cross-checking each others' results. The easternmost of the three lines continues to turn further east, down into the wooded slope; the central line goes almost straight ahead, unfortunately into dense hawthorn scrub barely a dozen yards (10m) or so from

131

the boundary wall. The third line continues west for a while, then suddenly veers northward in an almost straight line, as if along a rock-fissure, up the slight slope towards the dome of the north field. After about forty yards (35m) the dowsing response seems to become confused, and in effect stops in the same 'tangled' area identified in the somewhat abortive dowsing-work of the previous session in the north field. Once again, the lines are marked with flags at key-points, and recorded with photographs and sketch-diagrams.

The final stage is to track the apparent paths of the lines south-ward along the mound from where they 'enter' the false-portal. This part of the work is also as an independent crosscheck of a previous session here by Liz, so we revert to the previous work-pattern, with only Tom doing the dowsing, and Liz managing flags and notes. This is somewhat of a sprint, as the light is fading fast.

This time we *have* remembered to bring enough flags – almost a couple of hundred, in four different colours, yet we're still run-ning low by the time we get to the end of each trace. But the final results seem clear enough. At the least, they do seem to match with Liz's previous findings in that the lines run almost parallel down the length of the mound, after the two side-lines cross over each other – and the centre line – directly behind the portal.

Belas Knap – flags mark waterlines crossing above portal

We photograph the lines of marker-flags in the last of the dusk, then it's time to pack up and go. We say our goodbyes to the barrow, before squelching off down the soggy Cotswold Way back to the car. As usual, there's a clear sense, several times on the half-mile walk, of the barrow requiring our further attention, like a child wanting yet another 'last' goodbye-wave. By the time we do get to the car, we're both exhausted, and those sandwiches we'd saved are definitely needed. It's fortunate, too, that Liz is the 'designated driver' for this session: Tom had done most of the dowsing, all of it intense and unusually fast, so for a while he's an accurate example of the adage "don't dowse and drive"!

Wiggold, near Cirencester

This site is on private land, on a farm in the southern Cotswolds region of south-west England. Towards its southern end, this field contains a feature believed to be a Neolithic long-barrow, the subject of current archaeology research and excavation by a team from Bournemouth University led by Professor Tim Darvill. There's not much to see on the surface – in essence it's an almost-flat field, with stone walls and occasional sheep, and a couple of notches off one corner where some land has been sold off for house-gardens. It seems never to have been ploughed, though, so the archaeological record should be almost intact.

Wiggold field, August 2008

The purpose of this session was preparation for a site-visit during the annual conference of the British Society of Dowsers, which was planned to include a summary from Darvill's team, archaeology dowsing and Liz's work on archaeography.

Because the site is on private property, we've simplified the grid-references to just the last three digits (in metres), within the one-kilometre British National Grid square. For the full reference to the site's location, see the Bournemouth archaeology reports.

In the map-image, the effective record starts at waypoint 128, up in the northwest corner. Ignore the prior trace to the west of that point, as it only represents GPS 'warm-up' time; likewise the trace after waypoint 196. After completing a counter-clockwise circuit round the field (waypoints 128-194), we did a quick check of the barrow (waypoints 195-6) before being stopped by heavy rain.

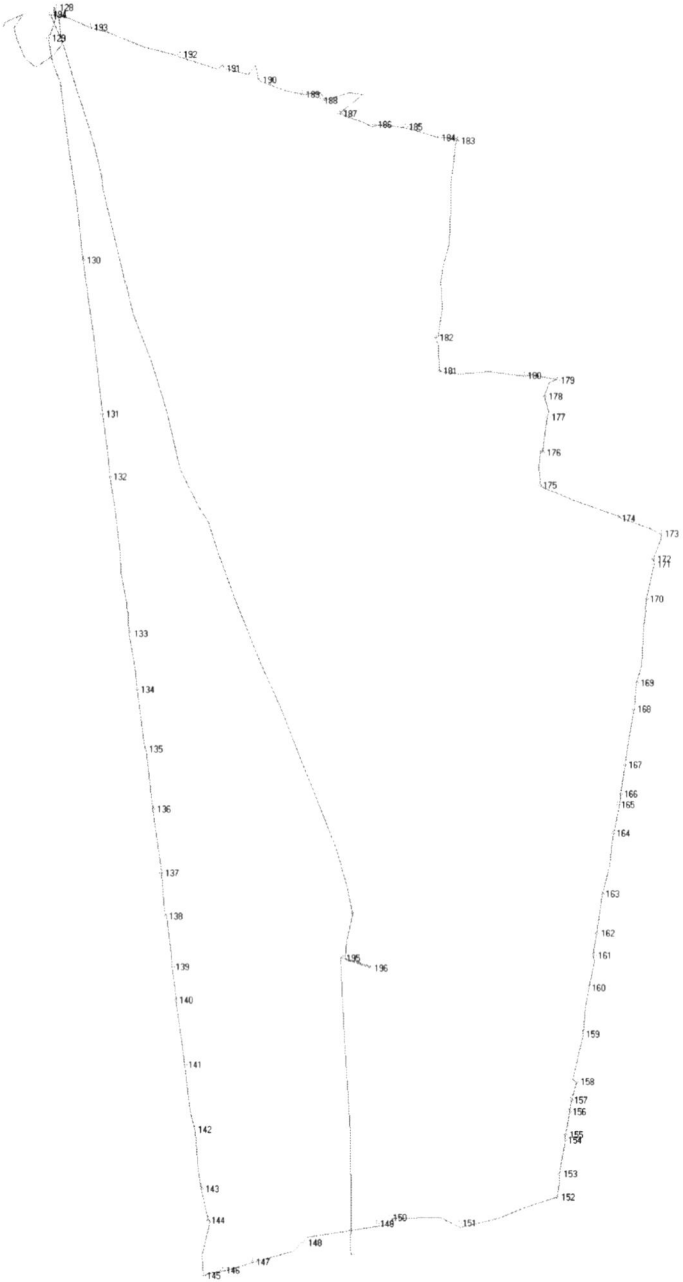

GPS trace, Wiggold Farm, 13 August 2008

ID	Comment	E N	Time
128	NW corner-post of field, close by main entrance gate to field	548 675	11:06:42
129	North post of gate (for traverse round the field, will typically walk c.6-10ft inside from fence to avoid long wet grass and other obstructions; the track will show a point at the corners where we go out to get the exact locations)	545 664	11:07:25
130	Edge of 'lumpy bit' (in energetic terms) coming from eastward in field	558 586	11:09:16
131	South post of old gate	565 531	11:10:54
132	Possible enclosed area? TG: headache Gully to W ('watery place'?) Becomes easier to breathe about 20 paces to S of 132	567 509	11:12:26
133	Gate post; 'light-hearted' feeling	575 454	11:15:04
134	Lower-back tingle; ESE within mound presence	577 435	11:15:59
135	Up-and-down energy, below knees / lower spine, moving	580 414	11:17:04
136	Feeling of being pulled back and down from lumbar spine	583 393	11:18:25
137	'Chemical smell'; feeling of pulled forward from knees	586 370	11:19:10
138	TG 'marching' feeling – LPW 'energy up to knees and down in rapid pulse'	588 354	11:19:51
139	Pushed to left from knees; TG 'stomach disrupted'	590 337	11:20:34
140	Whole-body tingle. spine-judder; TG: guts clearing, belching	592 325	11:21:17
141	TG: base-of-spine; LPW: feeling as if walked into a wire; breathing, letting go	595 302	11:22:27
142	TG: stomach tension; LPW: pushing against	598 279	11:23:16
143	TG: 'something', can't specify, disruptive, uncertain; LPW: 'need to run to edge of field to get over next bit quickly'	601 259	11:23:58
144	TG: 'neck push'; both: sense of 'sacred space', or more a 'no-go zone', should not be there, etc	603 248	11:24:45
145	Corner of stone wall at edge of field; 'heavy space' still	601 228	11:26:02
146	TG: 'becoming easier to breathe'	609 230	11:26:40
147	TG: 'sick feeling'; LPW: 'a waiting place'	619 233	11:27:07
148	Animal track over wall into woods	638 240	11:27:49
149	TG: 'open, bright'; LPW: 'sad feeling'	664 247	11:28:39
150	Animal track at post on wall	669 249	11:29:20
151	Really strong animal-track at angle NE out of wood	694 247	11:29:57
152	Edge of SE corner of field	729 256	11:31:11
153	Animal track from wood crosses over wall into E field	730 264	11:32:05

ID	Comment	E N	Time
154	TG: base-of-spine tension; LPW: back-jolt	732 276	11:32:53
155	Animal track over wall	732 278	11:33:17
156	TG: headache, tension in guts	733 286	11:33:44
157	Animal track over wall	734 290	11:34:02
158	Animal track over wall, heavy – suggests badger rather than deer; also TG: tension in gut	736 297	11:34:33
159	Animal track over wall	738 313	11:35:23
160	Sense of pressure, difficulty in breathing	740 329	11:35:48
161	Animal track over wall	742 341	11:36:24
162	Sense of meaning forced upright – propulsion forward	743 349	11:36:47
163	Animal track; TG: 'taste of tin', also guts	745 363	11:37:24
164	LPW: 'sad, tearful'; TG: 'disoriented, woolly'	748 385	11:38:13
165	'Movement through'	750 394	11:39:01
166	RED MARKER (presumably from Bournemouth archaeology survey?); also TG: base-of--spine	751 398	11:39:31
167	'Movement over?'	753 409	11:40:18
168	[starts 6 paces back, to S] Sense of 'big empty space'	756 428	11:40:59
169	End of 'big empty space'	757 437	11:41:34
170	LPW: 'sick feeling', also TG: 'taste of tin', 'eye-ache'; also animal track at post	761 466	11:42:26
171	Gatepost	764 479	11:43:18
172	Curved animal track; also 'sick feeling' at lump in ground rise	763 480	11:43:36
173	Edge of field – NE corner; also sick-feeling, headache	766 489	11:44:56
174	Headache eased off by this point	750 495	11:46:05
175	Edge of wall-post (internal corner in field)	722 506	11:46:53
176	Upper body pulled back – chest-pain	723 518	11:48:15
177	Walked over into hollow in field; also feeling of 'down'	725 530	11:48:58
178	Lower-body sensation	724 537	11:49:47
179	Another internal corner in field – animal track, may be human?	728 543	11:50:12
180	Animal track; also headache; disturbed ground, seems turned-over?	716 545	11:50:49
181	Corner-post for another internal corner in field; unusual large flat stone noted, approx 5ft from corner	686 546	11:51:47
182	Both: 'woozy, weird, all over the place', 'a churned-up mess' (feeling continues for both for remainder of this partial edge of the field)	685 558	11:53:02
183	Corner-point, with possible stile; prominent animal and/or human track; feeling 'exhausted'	692 629	11:55:09

ID	Comment	E N	Time
184	TG: strong sense of pushing-out of stomach; LPW: 'war-time feeling'	685 630	11:55:57
185	Animal track; edge of hollow in field; feeling of being pushed; LPW: 'bad feeling'	673 633	11:56:35
186	Sense of 'inside, enclosed', 'small and subdued', 'suppressed, subservient' *[3 paces later]* Out into hollow, 'feels odd'	662 634	11:57:27
187	Very strong sense of futility, 'why bother?'	650 638	11:58:44
188	In low of hollow, TG: sense of 'women's stuff' [in Aboriginal sense], a 'women's space'; LPW: [log shows small drawing / diagram of 'energy contained within', womb-like]; also animal-track in and out through wall	643 642	11:59:28
189	Difficulty in breathing; sense of 'a long way to go'	636 645	12:00:22
190	Animal track; also sense of relief, of having moved out of 'heavy space'	621 650	12:00:59
191	Sense of openness; also sense of bands across to opposite field *[see 130]*	608 654	12:01:42
192	Sense of having crossed boundary – turned OK 2 paces back; feeling of 'light-hearted'	592 659	12:02:33
193	Dark leaving edge? 'between wobble'	560 668	12:03:21
194	Back to start-point *[should be same as 128]* *(sensing not recorded in walk across field to nominal site of long-barrow)*	545 673	12:04:13
195	Dowsing for water-lines suggests blind-spring or equivalent (confirmed by both) also LPW: similar feeling as for forecourt at Belas Knap	652 340	12:18:52
196	Location of archaeology marker on barrow	662 336	12:19:21

Just visible at the top of the main map-image (p.134) is a sizeable GPS-anomaly, occurring between waypoints 186 to 192.

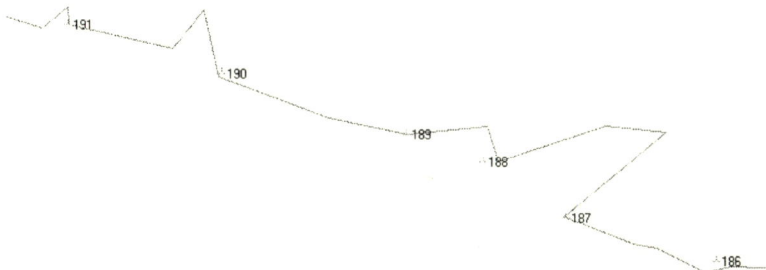

Detail of GPS anomaly, Wiggold Farm, 13 August 2008

The actual track walked there was almost a straight line, alongside a stone wall, with probably less than three feet (1m) actual deviation; but the GPS trace shows a deviation of up to about thirty-five feet (11m) north-east – a fair bit more than the ten-foot (3m) precision listed on the GPS at the time. Contrast this with the trace elsewhere on the circuit, which in general shows a reasonably smooth path relative to the waypoints, with all deviations well within the expected tolerances. (The deviations at the south end are to avoid obstructions at the edge of the wood.) As the sensings-records for those waypoints show, we passed through a small hollow here – the only one on the circuit, and probably less than two feet (0.6m) deep – and encountered perhaps the strangest and most unpleasant sensings of the circuit.

No idea what it means – if anything – but it's there for the record, anyway.

APPENDIX: RESOURCES

Books and text resources

Archaeography, deep mapping and local distinctiveness:

- Aaron Watson on archaeography and archaeoacoustics: see www.monumental.uk.com/
- Liz Poraj-Wilczynska on archaeography: see 'Liz PW's Belas Knap' at bk.lizpw.com
- Michael Shanks on archaeography: see www.archaeography.com/photoblog/
- Michael Shanks on deep mapping: see documents.stanford.edu/MichaelShanks/51 and metamedia.stanford.edu/~mshanks/projects/deep-mapping.html
- local distinctiveness and Parish Maps: see Common Ground, www.commonground.org.uk/distinctiveness/d-rules.html and www.commonground.org.uk/parishmaps/m-index.html

British Society of Dowsers Earth Energies Group, *An Encyclopaedia of Terms: suitable for those studying earth energies through dowsing* (British Society of Dowsers EEG, 2000 [2nd edition])

WIB Beveridge, *The Art of Scientific Investigation* (Heinemann Education, 1957)

Edward de Bono, *Practical Thinking* (Jonathan Cape, 1971)

Colin Clark: Sensitive Awareness Model, see www.drawninward.com

Sue Clifford, Angela King and others, *From Place to PLACE: maps and Parish Maps* (Common Ground, 1996)

Ramsey Dukes (pseudonym), *SSOTBME: an essay on magic, its foundation, development and place in modern life* (The Mouse That Spins, 1974 [revised e-book edition 2000])

C.A Fortlage, *Dowse, Survey and Record: an essential guide to simple surveying for dowsers* (private / British Society of Dowsers, 2006)

Dion Fortune, *Psychic Self-Defence* (Aquarian Press, 1988 [revised edition])

Tom Graves, *The Diviner's Handbook* (Destiny Books, 1976/2003)

Tom Graves, *The Dowser's Workbook* (Tetradian Books, 2008)

Tom Graves, *Elements of Pendulum Dowsing* (Tetradian Books, 2008)

Tom Graves, *Inventing Reality: towards a magical technology* (Grey House In The Woods, 2007 [2nd edition])

Tom Graves, *Needles of Stone: 30th anniversary edition* (Grey House In The Woods, 2008)

Tom Graves, *Power and Response-ability: the human side of systems* (Tetradian Books, 2008)

Tom Graves' website: see www.tomgraves.org and weblog.tomgraves.org

John Grinder and Richard Bandler, *The Structure of Magic: a book about language and therapy Vol.I* and *The Structure of Magic Vol.II* (Science and Behavior Books, 1989)

Keith Johnstone, *Impro: improvisation and the theatre* (Methuen, 1981)

Thomas Kuhn, *The Structure of Scientific Revolutions* (Chicago University Press, 1970)

Lucy Lippard, *Overlay: contemporary art and the art of prehistory* (The New Press, 1995 [revised edition])

John Michell, *The Old Stones of Land's End* (Elephant Press, 1973)

Hamish Miller and Paul Broadhurst, *The Sun and the Serpent* (Mythos, 1990)

Robert M Pirsig, *Zen and the Art of Motorcycle Maintenance* (Bodley Head, 1974)

Liz Poraj-Wilczynska's website: see www.lizpw.com

Colin Renfrew, *Figuring It Out: what are we? where do we come from? the parallel visions of artists and archaeologists* (Thames & Hudson, 2003)

Wikipedia summaries on Causal Layered Analysis, Cynefin, ISO-9000, Six Sigma and Total Quality Management: search on en.wikipedia.org/wiki/Main_Page

Societies

British Society of Dowsers: National Dowsing Centre, 2 St Ann's Road, Malvern, Worcestershire, WR14 4RG, UK; web: www.britishdowsers.org

American Society of Dowsers: PO Box 24, Danville, VT 05828 USA; web: www.dowsers.org

Printed in the United Kingdom by
Lightning Source UK Ltd., Milton Keynes
138325UK00002BA/6/P